A nostalgic look at

BIRMINGHAM TRAMS

1933-1953

Volume 3
The eastern and western routes
Including the Stechford routes,
the West Bromwich, Wednesbury and Dudley routes,
and the Smethwick, Oldbury and Dudley routes

David Harvey

Silver Link Publishing Ltd

This book is dedicated to the memory of John Stanford, a fellow member of
the Birmingham Transport Historical Group, who died shortly after the
publication of Volume 2 which he helped to edit.
A friend who is sorely missed.

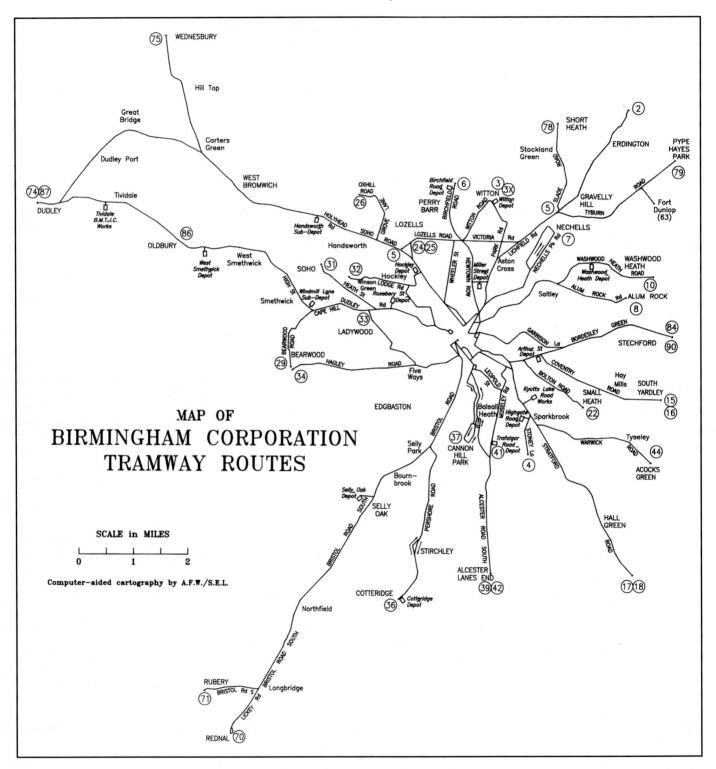

MAP OF BIRMINGHAM CORPORATION TRAMWAY ROUTES

SCALE in MILES

Computer-aided cartography by A.F.W./S.E.L.

Map of Birmingham Corporation tramway routes

This map shows the whole of the Birmingham tramway network, including the Stechford routes to the east and the western routes to Dudley via Oldbury and via West Bromwich. It does not purport to show the system at any given date, being intended to locate each route to scale and place it in its geographical location. Only the route numbers of regular all-day tramcar services are shown.

For detail of trackwork and locations of short-working turning points, see the definitive maps by J. C. Gillham, extracts of which are given in each chapter along with my own maps of the Black Country routes.

CONTENTS

ACKNOWLEDGEMENTS

THIS third volume of *A Nostalgic Look at Birmingham Trams* would once again not have been possible had it not been for all those tram enthusiasts and photographers whose work is credited within the main text.

I am extremely grateful to Roy Brook, the late W. A. Camwell, Ray Coxon, John Edgington, F. N. Lloyd Jones, T. Marsh, David Packer, L. W. Perkins, H. B. Priestley, Ray Wilson, W. J. Wyse and Alf Yates for allowing me access to their photographic collections and providing me with information and dates. Special thanks must be given to Stanley Webb whose knowledge of the Black Country routes was invaluable and whose unfailing help and knowledge was always available. Also to Geoffrey Morant, who was so instrumental in the initial stages of obtaining colour slides for all three volumes, and to Keith Terry, who was also a great help in tracing colour photographs.

Without the help of Peter Jaques this volume would not have been possible. His advice, helpful comments and his meticulous attention to detail have been of enormous value, and his enthusiasm for this project has been a source of great encouragement. I am extremely grateful for his assistance and to his wife Dorothy for putting up with my visits once a week when Peter and I have met to discuss and amend this volume.

I would also like to thank Norman Glover whose splendid photographs appear in this volume and whose reminiscences and proof-reading have been extremely useful.

My thanks also go to John Gillham for again allowing me to use extracts of his Birmingham track layout maps, to Stan Letts and Arthur Whitehouse for producing the excellent general layout map of the Birmingham tram system, and to Tony Hayward, who drove 2489 (JOJ 489), our preserved Birmingham Crossley double-decker bus, for the photographic reconstruction.

Special acknowledgement must be given to the late P. W. Lawson's book on the Birmingham Corporation Tramways Rolling Stock, and Archie Mayou's definitive work on tramcar allocations in Birmingham, as both works have been essential to the production of all three volumes of *A Nostalgic Look at Birmingham Trams*. I have not included a Bibliography as the list of secondary sources would almost fill a volume on its own! So to all the other authors on aspects of the local history of Birmingham and the surrounding areas may I offer my sincere thanks.

Finally, thanks must be given to my wife Diana who allowed me the time to research and produce this volume and whose critical comments and patience have been invaluable.

First published in October 1995

British Library Cataloguing in Publication Data

A catalogue record for this book is available from the British Library

ISBN 1 85794 037 7

Silver Link Publishing Ltd
Unit 5
Home Farm Close
Church Street
Wadenhoe
Peterborough PE8 5TE
Tel/fax 01832 720440

Printed and bound in Great Britain

FOREWORD

Sir Adrian Cadbury

THE HOUSE where I was born was on the corner of Hole Lane and the Bristol Road, directly opposite a tram stop. Trams, therefore, had an important place in my early life. I vividly remember the Silver Jubilee in 1935, because an illuminated tram was an exciting part of the celebrations.

I suspect that tram drivers hoped that no one would want to get off or on at Hole Lane, because it interfered with their headlong flight down the hill from Northfield when going towards town, or down the even steeper slope from Selly Oak on their way to the Lickey.

The trams rocked excitedly as they sped down those hills and it was always our hope as children that they might hit as they passed each other at the end of our

lane; but they never to my knowledge did. Their brakes, when they did come to an aggrieved halt at Hole Lane, provided another link with our family. My uncle Norman Cadbury did not make chocolate like my father, but ran the EMB company in West Bromwich, which made brakes for trams. He and my cousins lived in Weoley Park Road, just a tram stop nearer Selly Oak.

We travelled on the tram as children to go into town or out to the Lickey. When I was learning to play golf, I used to get off at Pebble Mill and walk on to the course via the drive of what was then the Bishop's house.

There is a satisfying certainty about trams; they can only follow their tracks. There were trams, to be avoided, that turned off at Pebble Mill, which was an interesting manoeuvre in itself. Otherwise there was no check to their progress out of town, apart from the stop in Selly Oak, where the crew filled their billy cans with tea. The occasional smothering fog of those days would effectively disrupt Birmingham's motor traffic, but the trams trekked on regardless. They had considerable merit as a mode of transport, their main drawback being that they picked up and set down their passengers in the middle of the road, at the mercy of the passing traffic.

I still have the odd penny, bent and flattened from being carefully inserted in the tram tracks, so that it would be run over. Our unspoken hope that one day something larger in the tracks might derail even so mighty a monster as a tram never came to pass. There was, on the other hand, the very occasional entertaining sight of a red Typhoo Tea van stuck in the tram tracks, at road crossings, because their unusually narrow wheels fitted happily into the groove where the tram wheels ran.

In my view trams have never received their due in literature. The only poem in which they feature, as far as I know, is one by Louis Macneice on Birmingham:

'On shining lines the trams like vast sarcophagi move.'

That was not how we saw them as children. The soothing clatter of passing trams was our background noise at home from early morning to the day's end. My bedroom looked out on to the Bristol Road, and when the trams ceased to run I missed their reassuring sound and did not sleep as well for quite a time.

INTRODUCTION

THE BIRMINGHAM tram system flourished through the first 30 years of the century, giving efficient, low-cost travel to the public. It made sufficient profit that for some of its period of operation the Tramways Department was able to put money back into the Council coffers and help to lower the rates bills of the citizens of Birmingham.

The system declined slowly from about 1930, when the closure of the first unprofitable arterial route, along Hagley Road, took place. Although no statement was ever made that the trams would go, by 1936 it had been made clear that any replacement infrastructure would be kept to a minimum and that new routes would be operated by buses. Had it not been for the Second World War, the trams would have gone by about 1944; they survived until 1953 because of the unavailability of new buses. Unlike many systems, high standards of maintenance were kept virtually to the end.

This third volume illustrates the routes to the eastern suburb of Stechford and the services within the city along Hagley Road, Soho Road and Dudley Road, as well as those services on the latter two roads that were taken over from BET operation into the Black Country. These routes represented very different operating conditions. The Handsworth routes with their bogie cars, operating an efficient high-speed service into the Black Country, were a very different proposition from the other Black Country route through Smethwick and Oldbury, which operated the oldest four-wheelers over the former Birmingham & Midland Tramways system. The Stechford route again exclusively used four-wheel trams on a route that perhaps deserved more modern trams, having one of the last reserved track sections to be opened in the city.

As in previous volumes, each route is covered by a pictorial survey from the city centre to the outer terminus, using where possible previously unpublished photographs. The early abandonment section in this volume covers the Hagley Road service, which was closed in 1930, as it fits into the geographical area covered by this volume.

The colour section, of necessity, shows a more general view of the last years of the Birmingham system as the routes covered in this volume pre-date easily available colour film.

On the last night of the Handsworth trams, bogie car 551 was the final tram from Wednesbury. At Carters Green its passengers were transferred to ex-Radial car 128, which is seen here in Whitmore Street in the early hours of Sunday 2 April 1939, surrounded by a crowd wishing to see the last tramcar return to Hockley depot and thereby witness the end of 50 years of tramcar operation in the Hockley and Handsworth areas.

Car 128 carries a small 'RIP' notice on the open-balcony wrought-ironwork and, as well as losing all its destination blinds, it returned to Hockley depot in darkness as souvenir hunters took all the light bulbs! It was due for withdrawal anyway, and by the following Thursday had been taken to West Smethwick yard to be broken up.

Route closures, after the abandonment of Stratford Road two years earlier, gradually became ceremonies involving the public. In 1937 car 564 was pulled into Highgate Road depot from the Stratford Road junction; after the war the other closures would become better publicised and attended until the chaotic scenes in July 1953 finally ended the system. *R. T. Coxon collection*

A BRIEF HISTORY OF BIRMINGHAM CORPORATION TRAMWAYS (1945-1953)

AT THE END of hostilities the tram system was in something of a run-down state. Forty-three trams had been damaged beyond repair in the air-raids during the war and four tram depots had received bomb damage. The Nechells trolleybus route had been closed on 30 September 1940 and from the end of 1941 no fewer than 67 trams had been repainted in wartime grey. A programme of dispersal from certain tram depots had taken place so that the risk of air-raid damage to the stock could be kept to a minimum. Services were cut back and the number of request stops were reduced and, where retained, moved 40 or so yards so that track wear could be evened out.

One of the first post-war jobs was to instigate track and overhead repairs throughout the tramway system and restore services to something like their pre-war standard. The damaged trams stored in Sampson Road Paint Shop along with the Nechells trolleybuses had to be quickly removed as the lease on the site was due to expire. In addition, the 22 trams of the 71 Class that had been held in reserve throughout the war were also sold for scrap.

It took nearly two years before the fleet was restored to a reasonable standard. All new overhauls after 1946 received a new simplified livery, with plain blue below the waist-rail and two blue bands between decks; this had been adapted from the bus livery, and although it had its critics, it did look very smart when freshly applied.

Abandonments resumed as soon as buses became available. Although the Transport Department had provisionally placed orders for new buses as early as 1942, obtaining them after the end of the war was extremely difficult and the first bus to arrive, 1481 (GOE 481), was not delivered until 20 June 1947.

The Lodge Road route was first to go, on 29 March 1947, when car 260 closed the route. As this was an isolated route operating the last of the 15 Brill-Maley cars, it did not affect the operation of the rest of the system.

The Ladywood route was next to be abandoned, on 30 August 1947, when cars 345 and 319 were drafted in from Miller Street to close the route; afterwards both were broken up. The displaced air-brake bogie cars of the 732 Class went to Selly Oak depot. This route closure led to the first depot, Rosebery Street, to give up its trams after the end of the war.

As the bus fleet itself was in a poor state, the next abandonment on the two Stechford routes, which had originally been intended for 1 April 1940, was delayed until there were enough new buses to operate the replacement bus services. The two Stechford routes, via Digbeth and Fazeley Street, were closed on 2 October 1948 along with the St Andrew's football specials, with car 316 having the distinction of being the last tram to enter Coventry Road depot. After that, only the trolleybuses were left to share the garage accommodation with the new Daimler CVD6s of the 1756 batch.

With this abandonment, the best of the 301 Class four-wheelers were redistributed to Miller Street, Washwood Heath and Witton depots, while those left at Coventry Road were run round to Moseley Road depot for storage and eventual scrapping.

During 1948 plans were drawn up for the complete closure of the tram system. Again the delivery of new buses was a vital factor in determining the programme. Additional remedial work was also necessary to keep the bogie-cars up to standard. From late 1947 until 1950, 57 tramcars, mainly of the 512 and 587 Classes, had their bodies rebuilt at Kyotts Lake Road Works. This involved strengthening the bodies with steel plates, which remedied the problems that had arisen during the course of over 20 years' operation. Other work at the same time included electrical re-wiring of the older bogie cars and general repair work that was going to be necessary to keep the trams running for the final five or so years of the system.

The first group of routes to close after the announcement of the plans for total tram abandonment were the Moseley and Kings Heath services. These had been provisionally listed for closure as long ago as 1938, but the original plan had to be considerably altered. The Moseley routes had the distinction of being the last narrow-gauge tram routes in the country to be worked all day by open-balconied four-wheel trams. These were the 401 Class, some of which were still being repainted as late as February 1949. The Moseley Road services ended on Saturday 1 October 1949 when car 386 closed the routes and all the 401 Class were withdrawn. Moseley Road depot was converted for buses, again Daimler CVD6s, but this time of the 1931 Class, and a similar number of pre-war Daimler COG5s.

The closure of the Perry Barr and Witton routes took place on Saturday 31 December 1949, when cars 13 and 18 respectively closed the services. It was also the last day that football specials were run by trams, and it was perhaps appropriate that Aston Villa lost! With these closures, the remaining trams of the 1-20 Class and the last ex-CBT trams, 451 and 452, were withdrawn; this left just 27 301 Class four-wheel trams in an otherwise all-bogie fleet. These surviving 301 Class trams would be eliminated with the next route closures.

On the following day, trams were parked at the Fox & Goose terminus, as they had been during the Second World War when it was used as a dispersal point. This time, however, it was because of the start of work to convert Washwood Heath depot for the next stage of the

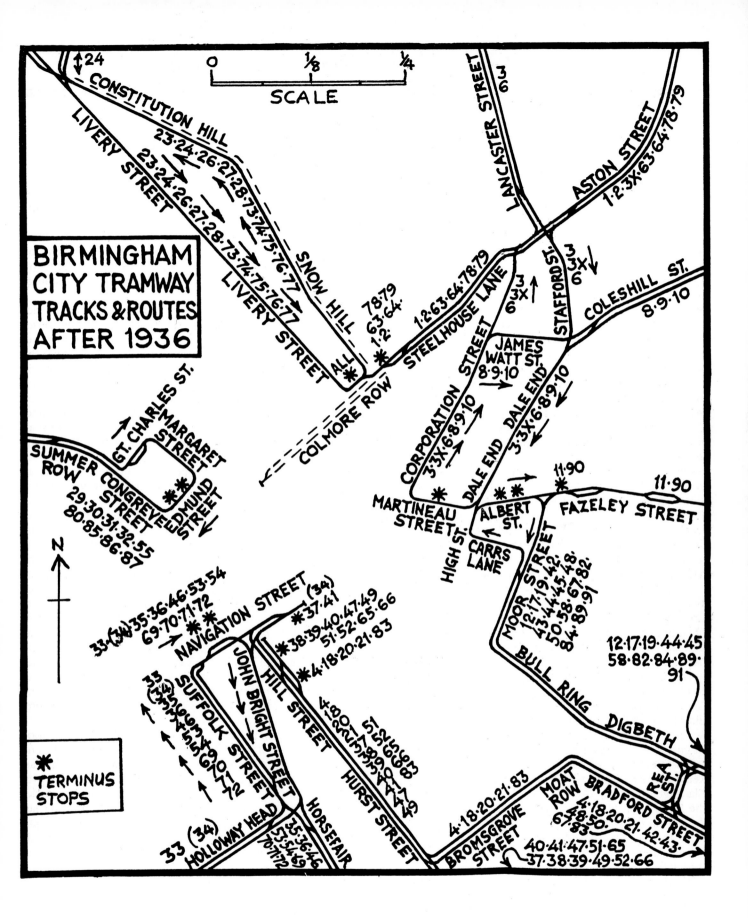

BIRMINGHAM
CITY TRAMWAY
TRACKS & ROUTES
AFTER 1936

TERMINUS
STOPS

conversion programme. This took place on Saturday 30 September 1950 when the Washwood Heath and Alum Rock services operated in the main by bow-collector-fitted 762 Class cars from Washwood Heath depot and the inter-suburban 5 route from Lozells to Gravelly Hill, operated by Witton depot, closed. The last trams on all these routes were 301 Class cars, 320 on the 45 route, 357 on the Alum Road route, and last of all 309, as the last number 10 and the last tram into Washwood Heath depot. The buses used in the conversion were mainly nearly new exposed radiator Crossleys.

Witton depot was now used only for scrapping trams after these closures, and all of the Washwood Heath bogies, by now equipped with trolley-poles, went to Selly Oak depot, which concentrated all the 110 air-brake 63 hp cars numbered from 732 at Selly Oak and Cotteridge to work the Bristol Road and Pershore Road services. Selly Oak also had about 38 magnetic brake cars while the remainder of the fleet, some 113 trams, were at Miller Street.

The fleet now settled down for 21 months, as the next conversion was the Coventry Road trolleybuses. These were abandoned because the majority of the fleet was due for renewal, and, with only a total of 74 trolleybuses in a fleet of about 1,800 buses, they were non-standard. Trolleybuses were abandoned on Saturday 30 June 1951 with Coventry Road garage now only operating motor buses. Kyotts Lake Road Works completed the last tram repaints that year; after that trams only visited the works for touching-up and mechanical work.

Buses took over the Bristol and Pershore Road routes after the abandonment on Saturday 5 July 1952. From the previous August preparatory work had taken place at both Selly Oak and Cotteridge depots. Tram 757 was converted to a cleaner's room and Daimler COG5 bus 1222 (FOF 222) was used as a crew room at Selly Oak. As usual, up to 18 trams were parked on the Rednal loop at night.

The last new pieces of track were put in Pebble Mill road, when three new cross-overs were laid in order that trams could be parked on the inbound track to make room in both depots during the conversion. Car 800 closed the Cotteridge route and the last tram into Selly Oak was car 777. Brand new Daimler CVG6s and Guy 'Arab' IVs replaced the trams. After the tram routes were closed 54 tramcars had to be stored on the reserved track between Pebble Mill Road and Eastern Road for up to nearly three weeks. Car 513 was the last tram to be driven away on 23 July to Witton depot for scrapping. The two Cotteridge Lightweight trams, 842 and 843, were also withdrawn in connection with this penultimate abandonment.

With the closure of the reserved track along Bristol Road, the pride of the BCT tram system had gone, leaving only the Erdington group of routes on the north side of the city. It was considered not to be worthwhile to re-train the Miller Street drivers in air-brake operation, so the decision was made to keep the all-electric cars in service, for although they were older, their bodies were in better condition.

This still left a sizeable fleet of 127 trams available for service, of which 115 were crammed into Miller Street depot. After 30 November 1952, any 30 cars were stabled at Witton depot so that the conversion of Miller Street could take place, but there was no specific allocation.

The trams were still very much in evidence during the Coronation celebrations of June 1953, but this national event and its celebrations, with flag-bedecked buildings, was the last major event that the trams would see. On Sunday 28 June cars 616 and 623 were being used on the last tour of the remnants of the system and on the following Friday 36 cars went on the one-way journey from Miller Street to Kyotts Lake.

The last day of tramcar operation in the city was Saturday 4 July 1953. The services to Erdington, Short Heath and Pype Hayes ran as normal, with 66 trams available for use. In mid-morning, inbound trams stopped near Victoria Road and their passengers were transferred to waiting buses. The last car on the 78 route was 578, on the 79 it was 569, and the last service car on the 2 route from Erdington was car 690.

Then came the last rites with a smart-looking car 623 leaving Miller Street for the Steelhouse Lane terminus. It was followed by 616, crudely painted with 'BIRMINGHAM'S LAST TRAM' along both sides and 'THE END' on both dash panels. Both trams carried civic dignitaries and Transport Department employees and went to Erdington and back to the depot. The route was lined with people paying their last respects to the trams, but by 1.00 pm it was all over and the last tram had carried its last passenger!

Later that afternoon another 24 trams passed from Miller Street to Kyotts Lake Road, with car 679 being the last to coast down Carrs Lane from High Street to Moor Street as the wires had been removed in the spring of 1952. The police would not allow the convoy of trams to run down Albert Street to Moor Street during the day against the one-way flow of traffic, which is why this complicated arrangement took place on the last Friday and Saturday evenings. The last passenger cars were moved on the following Tuesday when nine trams went from Miller Street to Witton for scrapping.

On Saturday 6 August 1953 car 597 became the final tram to be broken up. Later the same afternoon, PW 8, which had been used as the works shunter, was driven out of Kyotts Lake Road Works, photographed and loaded on to a lorry to be taken to Bird's yard in Stratford for scrapping.

Birmingham Corporation trams had served the city for 49 years. For over 30 years the system's trams had been at the forefront of the development of modern tramcar equipment and had outlived the trolleybuses, which briefly threatened to replace them. Despite being restricted to narrow gauge, the tall, thin and somewhat stately trams in Birmingham had made a significant contribution to the growth of the city; they had also played an important role in tramcar operation and development in this country. They had contributed to the General Rate Fund by being consistently in profit and had made cheap travel available within the city.

There can be no greater tribute to the trams than this epitaph. On Whit Monday, 18 May 1937, Dudley Zoo opened, and it is estimated that a quarter of a million people travelled to Dudley, at least half by way of the two tram routes, either via West Bromwich or Oldbury. At 11.00 pm there were still 15,000 people to be taken back towards Birmingham, but the trams kept running until the demand for them had been met!

EARLY ABANDONMENTS

Hagley Road

THE HAGLEY ROAD route was opened on Friday 5 September 1913 and closed on Tuesday 9 September 1930, making it the penultimate arterial tram route to open in Birmingham and the third tram route to close.

The route was authorised by Royal Assent on 7 August 1912, but it was not opened without considerable opposition. The Hon Mrs Anstruther-Gough-Calthorpe, owner of the nearby Calthorpe Estate, objected most strongly, while Neville Chamberlain, the MP for Edgbaston, stated that 97 per cent of the residents were against the trams running along Hagley Road. The feeling of the 'carriage-folk' of the suburb was that their thoroughfare would be spoiled by the unsightly tramway overhead and street furniture and that as a result the whole tone of the area would be lowered.

In response to suggestions from certain members of the public who lived in the Edgbaston area and were aware of similar services in Liverpool, the Birmingham Transport General Manager, Alfred Baker, suggested a three-month experimental First Class service using the newest trams. Originally cars 581 to 586 were to be used, but in the event only 581 to 584 were needed. The First

The view over New Street station from the Central Grammar School in Suffolk Street in about 1928 shows a city that has certain landmarks that have survived to the present day. On the skyline is the Parish Church of St Martins, while the building in the foreground on the right survives today and houses a number of restaurants. The street pattern is also recognisably the same today, although Queens Drive, separating the huge canopy of the former LNWR side of New Street station from the curved roofs of the Midland Railway side, disappeared in the 1960s' rebuilding. In the middle of the entrance of Queens Drive, in Hill Street, just visible, is a Finlays tobacconists.

The two trams in the right foreground are on Bristol Road duties and will follow the track round to the right into John Bright Street. They are among the seven trams in Navigation Street, out-numbering the solitary ADC 507 bus, which can be seen below the steam and smoke coming from a departing locomotive.

The real interest in this photograph is that it might show a Hagley Road tram at its city terminus. The two furthest trams are loading up at the unusual central loading island at the corner of the Queens Hotel. There was no kerb-side loading here as trams from Kings Heath, Ladywood and the 34 service stopped at a double terminal stub that had the shelter behind it in the middle of the road. *D. R. Harvey collection*

Class passengers were carried only in the lower saloon, where the seats were covered with blue-plush cushions and the floors with rubber matting. The seating capacity downstairs was reduced from 28 to 24 and double fares were charged for the privilege of travelling in the added luxury.

Initially the First Class service ran along Hagley Road only as far as Fountain Road, while the normal service trams ran to the terminus at the Kings Head. Although it ran for the full three months allocated for the experiment, it was not a financial success; it could not entice passengers away from the LNWR's Harborne Railway, which took commuters into New Street Station, while the 'carriage-folk' of Edgbaston simply had little need for the service.

An unusual allocation took place when at least one of the two ex-CBT bogie cars, 451 and 452, which had been cut down to single-deckers, was used on the Hagley Road service.

The route became uneconomic, with the service competing in its inner part to Five Ways with the Ladywood tram route and beyond Five Ways along Hagley Road with parallel Corporation bus routes. The introduction of the Sandon Road buses on 29 September 1926 and the Portland Road service on 26 September 1927 made further inroads into the viability of the 34 tram route, as the buses were more frequent. The removal of the city terminus from the east end of Navigation Street to the west end, further away from the city centre, on 23 September 1929 was a further disadvantage, and with later service cuts the early closure of the Hagley Road trams became inevitable.

The route was originally lettered H and started from the Queens Hotel end of Navigation Street, although for the last year of operation it was moved to the Suffolk Street end. The route followed the Ladywood service along John Bright Street and turned right into Holloway Head, climbing up the steep hill to Bath Row. Here it crossed into Islington Row at Five Ways station before reaching the clock and the Joseph Sturge statue at Five Ways. The route then turned left into Hagley Road and gently climbed for the next 2 miles, through an area of large Victorian and Edwardian villas. It passed over the Harborne Railway branch, which was only about 100 yards short of the temporary First Class terminus at Fountain Road. The 34 route then descended to its terminus at the Kings Head public house at Lordswood Road. To the right, but never connected, was the 29 route from Bearwood to Smethwick and the city via Dudley Road.

For a map of the Hagley Road route, see page 15.

Below After leaving the city terminus at the Queens Hotel end of Navigation Street, the route to Hagley Road traversed John Bright Street before turning right across The Horsefair and up the steep climb of Holloway Head to Bath Row. Bath Row, running from Granville Street to Islington Row, was a Regency housing development that changed picturesque country lanes into symmetrical street patterns. By the mid-19th century town planning of this sort had given way to cramming as many people as possible into as small an area as possible. By the 1920s, when this photograph was taken, Bath Row, as a residential area, was displaying all the characteristic signs of an old area in terminal decline.

On the Broad Street side of the thoroughfare were all the interesting public buildings. In the distance can just be seen the 'wedding-cake', Ionic-porticoed tower of St Thomas's; this is all that is left of the church as its nave was destroyed by a bomb on 25 October 1940. The surrounding churchyard is now part of an International Peace Garden that was dedicated in 1994.

The tram on the extreme right is possibly car 517, still in open balcony condition, and is working out of the city on the Hagley Road service. This Rosebery Street-allocated tramcar is passing the Davenports Brewery site and will shortly reach the Queens Hospital, opened in 1841. It later became better known as the Birmingham Accident Hospital and was finally closed in 1992. The houses to the extreme left belong to the early Victorian period when residential property was still being built for the better-off, unlike the back-to-back housing found nearby in Lee Bank Road. *Commercial postcard*

Above right On reaching the end of Bath Row the trams turned right into Islington Row and climbed the steady gradient up towards Five Ways. These two trams are approaching the junction where stood the Five Ways clock, dedicated to the memory of a Mr Davies who had been the first District Coroner. The Kings Head-bound trams turned in front of the classically styled Lloyds Bank into Hagley Road, while the 33 tram route to Ladywood took the right-hand fork and crossed Broad Street into Ladywood Road.

Commercial postcards are always difficult to date, but this one does give a number of clues. The leading tramcar approaching the junction is one of the 512-586 Class. It appears to be one of the first eight of the Class, which entered service during October 1913 only one month after the opening of the Hagley Road route. The second tram is devoid of advertisements and appears to be one of the First Class service 512 Class trams introduced in 1914. The style of the clothes worn by the two children standing outside Lloyds Bank and the knickerbocker trousers worn by the boy standing in Islington Row further suggest a pre-First World War scene.

Only the Lloyds Bank building remains in its original position today. The clock was moved in the 1980s to stand outside the Swallow Hotel, formerly the office headquarters of ICI, on the corner of Harborne Road and Hagley Road. The houses in Islington Row on the right were replaced in the early 1920s by a rather attractive row of Art Deco-style shops that still remain today alongside what is now a dual-carriageway. *Commercial postcard*

Middle right In the last year of peace before the outbreak of the First World War, changes in the urban landscape and in the way of life had continued to evolve at a pace to which individuals could relate. Eventually nearly everything in this scene would disappear.

The two schoolgirls on the right, laden down with satchels and bags, cross Hagley Road and its tram tracks as the Southampton-registered cycle-car turns towards Islington Row. Facing it is an almost new tram 513, a United Electric Car-bodied 62-seat vestibuled bogie car. It is carrying, over the open balcony, the flop-over destination boards NAVIGATION STREET TO HAGLEY ROAD, and will take the Hagley Road tracks in the foreground. The large statue, which was unveiled in 1862 in the presence of a

crowd of 12,000 people, is of Joseph Sturge. He was a 19th-century Quaker who struggled for universal male suffrage and for the development of the Chartist ideals of Birmingham's first Member of Parliament, Thomas Attwood. He also set up the first adult education classes in the town for factory workers in 1845.

Just visible to the left of the statue is a Midland Red Tilling-Stevens TTA1, 30 hp petrol-electric bus. Built in 1912, this one, registered O 8201, was one of 30 buses taken over by Birmingham Corporation Tramways on 5 October 1914 under an agreement reached with the Birmingham & Midland Omnibus Company. This protected all Corporation tram and bus routes within the city boundary from Midland Red competition. The bus, still in Midland Red ownership, is working on the Corporation Street, New Street and Five Ways service. *Commercial postcard*

Below right The Hagley Road tram route to the Kings Head at Bearwood was opened on Friday 5 September 1913, but not without considerable opposition. As early as 17 October 1911 a meeting of objectors was held at the Plough & Harrow Hotel, just behind the photographer on the left of this 1913 view along Hagley Road looking towards Five Ways.

One objector, a Mr Combridge, said: 'Edgbaston wanted motor buses not trams. Trams would wreck a beautiful boulevard and spoil Edgbaston. Well-to-do folk would leave the area.' He also added that 'the brain workers of Birmingham lived largely in the Hagley Road district and naturally required peace and quiet'!

Car 389, a four-wheel, open-balconied tram, is working along Hagley Road towards Five Ways. This tramcar, and up to 20 others of the 361 Class, was briefly used on the new Hagley Road service until sufficient of the 512 Class of bogie trams had been delivered to Rosebery Street. This had been completed by about November 1913. *Commercial postcard*

HAGLEY RD EDGBASTON

Below This early 1920s scene shows one of Rosebery Street depot's 512 Class cars working the 34 route towards the city. The route numbering scheme was adopted in 1915 and the canopy roller-blind route boxes were installed after 1918, although it took a number of years to equip all the tramcar fleet. It appears that the tram has been fitted with side destination frames, which replaced the side slipboards at about the same time.

The tram is passing the Roman Catholic Oratory Church of the Immaculate Conception, the dome of which can be seen behind the Gothic-styled church house on the corner of Plough & Harrow Road. The church, largely hidden by the school buildings, was built in the Italian Renaissance style between 1903 and 1906 as a memorial to Cardinal John Henry Newman.

The tram has left the Ivy Bush junction and has now entered the half-mile of straight track that will taken the route to Five Ways. It is at about the same place as the previous photograph, but looking in the opposite direction. *Commercial postcard*

Middle left During the first year of operation of the service to the Kings Head, intending passengers wait to board or stride purposefully towards eight-wheel, open-balconied car 517, built by the United Electric Car Co Ltd (UEC) of Preston, inbound at Portland Road. It stands at the stop, with its superb pair of gas street lights mounted on a highly decorated sewer ventilation pipe, before travelling to the distant shops clustered around the Ivy bush junction at Monument Road.

Just visible above the trees to the left is the Baptist Church of the Redeemer, with its large central octagonal tower built to the design of James Cubitt in 1881.

Car 517 was at the beginning of 38 years of service life. It was finally withdrawn on 5 July 1952, by which time it had been totally enclosed, re-motored from its original Dick, Kerr DK19A 40 hp motors to GEC WT32R motors with an output of 70 hp, and had covered well over one million miles in service. *Commercial postcard*

Below left Hagley Road was lined with large Victorian and Edwardian houses that reflected the wealth of the householders. To the south, on the left of this out-of-town view, was the Calthorpe Estate, whose trustees had strong ideals about urban development; they saw that by planning development they could retain the air of gentility that was lacking when other Birmingham families, such as the Edwards family of Balsall Heath, sold off land for development.

Geographical urban models of the growth patterns of British cities always have the better housing, often owned by the factory owners, facing the prevailing fresh westerly winds. The factories and the artisans who worked in them lived in the cheaper, more polluted areas of the east. Birmingham was no exception - the most expensive housing within the city is still on the western approaches in the Edgbaston area.

This view of Hagley Road at St Augustines Road is towards the Kings Head and shows everything to do with trams except the tramcars! It was taken between September 1926 when bus 181 (OP 210), an AEC 504 with a Short Brothers 52-seat open-staircase body, was placed in service, and 9 August 1930, when the Hagley Road trams were replaced by buses. The bus entered service in the same month as the 6 bus route to Sandon Road was introduced. *Commercial postcard*

Right Standing at the compulsory stop at Fountain Road is UEC bogie car 582. Closer examination shows that the tram is one of the four 512-586 Class that when new were used on the experimental First Class service along Hagley Road; just visible are the brown curtains that were supposed to add a touch of luxury.

This service began on Wednesday 25 February 1914, but unlike the contemporary Liverpool operation, where nine routes and a total of 68 tramcars were converted, the Birmingham First Class scheme was on a much smaller scale using only four of the newest bogie cars.

The First Class tram service ran as far as Fountain Road, some 5 furlongs short of the normal terminus at the Kings Head public house; operation began after 8.30 am when it was superimposed on to the normal full service. However, cars 581 to 584 were allocated to the new Highgate Road depot and not to Rosebery Street, as it was felt that it was easier to keep them cleaner at the former depot. *A. D. Packer collection*

Right The young woman pushing a child in the perambulator begins to cross Sandon Road as the driver of four-wheel car 383 waits for the elderly man to alight after his short journey from the Kings Head terminus some half a mile away. Hagley Road, again totally devoid of traffic, has, in the intervening years since this 1914 photograph was taken, hardly changed at all; the majority of the large houses as exemplified by the one on the extreme left still remain. Car 383, built in the first month of 1912, was only used for the first few months of the Hagley Road service until the new 512 bogie cars became available. *W. A. Camwell collection*

Below right The terminus of the Hagley Road route was at the Kings Head public house at the crossroads of Lordswood Road and Bearwood Road. The Kings Head was rebuilt for the Holte Brewery Company between 1903 and 1905. The Calthorpe family were generally against allowing the building of licensed premises on their developments in Edgbaston, but because the site had been occupied by an inn since the reign of King George III they had little choice. In 1995 the hostelry was transformed into a 'theme pub' called 'The Quantum Experience'! The 29 service to Bearwood terminated at a stub terminus in Bearwood Road just beyond the junction that the mother and her son are approaching on the left.

Various attempts were made by the British Electric Traction Company to build a tram route to Halesowen. The route would have turned left off Beech Lanes, in the foreground, and gone via Bearwood and Cape Hill to Birmingham. The Halesowen Light Railway Order made it possible to link up with the BET-owned Bearwood line after protracted negotiations between the local authorities of Birmingham, Smethwick, Oldbury, Halesowen and Rowley Regis. The only line that was actually built, however, was the Hagley Road route, which was part of a seven-point plan to put trams into Harborne as well as to construct a tram depot in Earls Court Road, Harborne.

Bogie car 532 has just arrived at the terminus. The black rectangular box above the trolley-pole houses a light to assist the rewiring of the tramcars. The tram has a destination route 34 on the open-balcony route box, which suggests that the view was taken in the early 1920s; this is also confirmed by the style of the clothes worn by the women in the photograph. *Commercial postcard*

DUDLEY VIA SMETHWICK AND OLDBURY

THE HISTORY of the services from Birmingham to Dudley by way of Smethwick and Oldbury began when the Birmingham & Midland Tramways Company was formed on 22 November 1883. This was to take over the lines to be constructed by the Birmingham & Western District Tramways company outside the Birmingham boundary on Dudley Road and those lines leased from Birmingham Corporation within the town's boundary, with the exception of the proposed Heath Street route, which although laid was never operated in steam tram days. The lease on the lines within the boundary was held until June 1906.

On 6 July 1885 the B&MT opened its first steam tram line from Lionel Street along Dudley Road to the town boundary at Grove Lane. By 30 August 1885 the line had been extended to Smethwick and to Oldbury, with an hourly steam tram service to Dudley station. Although not directly involved with the later operation by Birmingham Corporation, there were two other branch lines; these were both from West Bromwich, one going along Spon Lane and the other via Bromford Lane to Oldbury. Such was the poor level of traffic generated on both of these steam-operated services that by 20 May 1893 arrangements had been made with Mr B. Crowther of West Bromwich to operate a horse tram service on both routes.

In August 1899 the BET obtained control of the B&MT with the intention of electrifying the lines. In February 1902 an agreement was reached with Birmingham City Council that enabled the company to convert and operate the line with electric traction between Summer Row and the boundary until the lease ran out in June 1906.

The 8-mile line to Dudley opened for electric traction on 21 November 1904, as well as a newly constructed branch from Cape Hill to Bearwood. The Soho branch along Heath Street was opened on 31 December 1904 and was extended over company-owned tracks to Soho station on 24 May 1905.

On 30 June 1906 the lease on the section within the

A general layout map of Black Country routes.
BDPT - Birmingham District Power & Traction Company Ltd
DS&DET - Dudley, Stourbridge & District Electric Traction Co Ltd
SSTC - South Staffordshire Tramways Company
WBCBC - West Bromwich Corporation Borough Council
WDET - Wolverhampton District Electric Tramways Co

Above right The Hagley Road route, and the Dudley route as far as Cape Hill, Smethwick, with branches to Soho and Bearwood.

Right Smaller-scale continuation of the Dudley route via Smethwick and Oldbury.

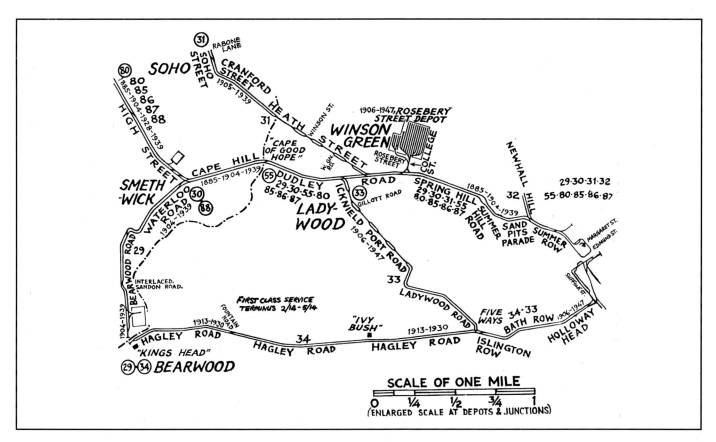

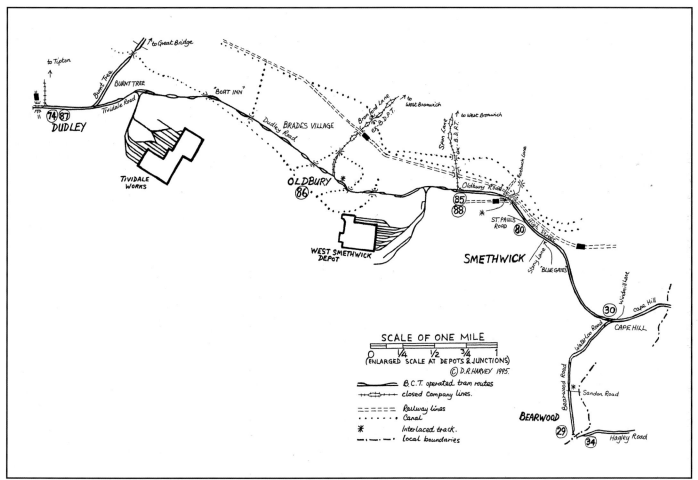

city expired and on the following day Corporation tram-cars began a joint service on the Bearwood and Soho routes. A new workshop for B&MT was opened at Tividale on 1 January 1907. On 13 August 1912 the company changed its name to the Birmingham District Power & Traction Company Ltd. A programme of track relaying and doubling as well as the replacement of centre-poles with span wires was undertaken in the years prior to the outbreak of war.

The Corporation-operated routes were given numbers in 1915, Bearwood becoming 29, Windmill Lane 30 and Soho 31. On 1 April 1928, after negotiations between Birmingham Corporation and Birmingham District, the Corporation would operate the Birmingham-Smethwick-Oldbury-Dudley route. Although the lease on the line had until 1938 to run and the operation was profitable, it must have been felt by the Company that it could not justify tramcar replacement costs for just a ten-year period. Having agreed to take over the services, the Corporation was so short of trams that they hired the existing fleet of 38 four-wheel, double-deck trams from BD for nearly four months until the delivery of the new Corporation 762-811 Class enabled the ex-Radial 71 Class trams to be released to operate the acquired services. The route to Dudley was numbered 87, with the main short-working as far as Oldbury being numbered 86.

The Company's tramways in Smethwick, Oldbury, Rowley Regis and Tipton were compulsorily purchased by those local authorities under the terms of the Tramways Act (1870) as from 1 January 1939. The Company's lease from Dudley Corporation also expired at the same time. Birmingham City Transport entered into an agreement with the Black Country Local Authorities of Smethwick, Oldbury, Rowley Regis, Tipton and Dudley to continue operation for another year. Eventually the decision to abandon the routes had to be taken; not only was the track outside the Birmingham boundary in a poor state, but also the local authorities wished to be rid of the trams. An agreement was made with the BMMO company to operate on behalf of the local authorities outside the boundary, and an operation agreement was made with BCT at the end of July 1939 regarding joint service arrangements that effectively continued the same sort of joint working that had been used on the trams prior to 1928.

With the declaration of war on 3 September, it seemed that the route might be reprieved, but the abandonment plans were continued and the final part of the once-huge Black Country tramway system closed on 30 September 1939.

The main line started in Birmingham, initially in Summer Row at Lionel Street, but in 1906 this was extended nearer to the heart of the city to a terminus at the rear of the impressive Council House in Edmund Street. On turning right into Congreve Street, the trams passed over the Birmingham Canal bridge and into Summer Row, dropping downhill to the Parade. This was the edge of the Jewellery Quarter and it was here that the Lodge Road trams on the 32 route turned right into Newhall Hill. The small row of shops in the Parade gave way to enamelling and paint industries, leading to the slight climb up in Sandpits and into Summer Hill Road, which was dominated by the large Bulpitts kitchenware factory.

The junction with Icknield Street marked the end of the inner city industrial area, for once into Spring Hill the main road was fronted by small shops that served the mid-Victorian back-to-backs, courtyards and terraces in this area on the edge of Ladywood and Hockley. Halfway up the hill to the right was College Street; this led to Rosebery Street depot, which operated all the Corporation workings on the Dudley Road services as well as the Ladywood and Lodge Road routes. This large 12-road depot had a capacity of 85 trams, and its entrance seemed to dominate the dingy area around it.

At the top of the hill the trams crossed the Soho Loop by way of Spring Hill Bridge before passing Dudley Road Hospital. Almost immediately the wide Lee Bridge over the Birmingham Canal Navigation's deep cutting, with the LNWR's main railway line from New Street running alongside, was crossed.

The road to the right, parallel to the cutting and flanked by rows of three-storeyed houses, was Heath Street, along which the 31 service ran, negotiating three passing loops. Just beyond Winson Green Road, where the prison could be glimpsed in the distance to the right, was the Birmingham-Smethwick boundary and the GKN factory straddling Cranford Street. Once at the end of Heath Street the trams regained a double-track section in an area of Victorian tunnel-backs and shops in Cranford Street before reaching Soho Street and the run to the terminus at Soho station.

Back at Lee Bridge and the Lee Bridge Tavern on the corner of Dudley Road and Heath Street, the trams entered a busy shopping centre. The first main road on the south side in this section was Icknield Port Road, where the 33 route terminated. Almost opposite this was Winson Green Road, which was crossed about half a mile away by the Lodge Road trams on their way to the terminus at Foundry Road. Just beyond this junction was Dudley Road Police Station, then Summerfield Park, the first piece of greenery seen since leaving the city centre.

The Dudley Road trams continued out of the city through a long row of shops and dropped downhill to Grove Lane, which is the City Boundary, marked by the Cape of Good Hope public house and the Mitchells & Butlers brewery. It was also the terminus of the 55 route, and beyond this point the trams were on Company-owned tracks.

Passing the brewery on the left, the trams continued up Cape Hill and into another main shopping centre clustered around the Windmill Lane and Waterloo Road junctions. This was the terminus of the 30 short-working and was where the Bearwood service, 29, branched off the main line and ran through an area of late Victorian houses and into Bearwood Road. Here it passed through a short section of interlaced track near the Three Shires Oak Road shops at the junction with Sandon Road, before running to the terminus only a few yards from the BCT Hagley Road line.

The main-line route left Cape Hill by way of High Street, passing the old steam tram coke yard at Windmill Lane before descending to Victoria Park and Smethwick Council House. The route reached the Blue Gates public houses in the middle of another half-mile-long Victorian shopping centre, which ran parallel to the south-west of the LNWR main line. The very busy High Street was originally a series of loops, but was doubled in 1914 to this point; by 1920 this had been continued to the Spon Lane junction, except for the short interlaced section over the GWR railway bridge. At the far end of High Street was St Paul's Road, the short-working terminus of the 80 route.

Once beyond Galton Bridge and Smethwick Junction railway station, the landscape changed from the late Victorian terraces to a very heavily industrialised area. Spon Lane was the 85 route terminus, and 200 yards beyond it was the Birmingham & Midland's West Smethwick depot; this had a capacity for 44 trams but did have a large depot yard in front of the 11-road car shed.

Almost immediately the line crossed Titford Canal branch and climbed through the narrow streets into Oldbury town centre. Passing along the signal-light-controlled section of track in Birmingham Street, the trams went through the Market Place; this was the terminus of the 86 service.

The route then descended a long straight section of track to Brades Village, a cluster of houses surrounded by derelict land and spoil heaps from abandoned coal mines. Although this section of the route along Dudley Road East was straight, the road was subject to subsidence. On reaching the Boat Inn, the trams turned left and climbed over the steep bridge of the Birmingham Canal into the more prosperous industrialised area of Tividale. At the Dudley end of Dudley Road West, the route passed the BMT's Tividale Works before climbing again to Burnt Tree junction where it met the former South Staffordshire tram route from Handsworth and West Bromwich. The two services then followed the common route to the terminus of the 87 service opposite Tipton Road on the railway bridge at Dudley station.

City Centre to Lee Bridge

In 1938 car 72, numerically the second of the ex-Radial trams of 1906, waits to turn out of Margaret Street into Edmund Street when working on the Bearwood service during 1938. Dominating the scene is the School of Arts and Crafts begun in 1883 as part of the 19th-century redevelopment of this area with important civic buildings. The building was financed by Louisa Anne Ryland who had earlier donated the land for Cannon Hill Park to the town of Birmingham. The main facade of the Art School is covered in red brick, terracotta, tiles and mosaic in an Art Nouveau extravaganza.

The 1936 Standard Flying Twenty parked on the corner of Cornwall Street is quite unusual for that date because it is painted in what appears to be cream, when the majority of British-built cars were painted in more sober colours, which usually meant black. *R. T. Wilson*

On Saturday 23 September 1939, with the war nearly three weeks old and the Oldbury tram routes with only one week to go before abandonment, car 301 is standing at the same spot as car 72 in the previous photograph, waiting to move on to the loading stands in Edmund Street. This tram had moved from Selly Oak depot in early April 1939 to replace 71 Class cars, and would itself have soon been withdrawn had the Stechford routes, which were scheduled to be the next stage of the tramway abandonment, not been reprieved. The sandbags are already in place against the rear of the Council House, while the kerbs have been painted black and white to assist drivers in the blackout. *J. S. Webb*

The terminus for all the Dudley Road routes was in Edmund Street, where trams stood alongside the Corporation Water Department offices, which formed part of the City Museum & Art Gallery block, opened in 1885 by Edward, Prince of Wales. This had been designed by Yeoville Thomason, who had previously designed the Council House in nearby Victoria Square.

On Tuesday 30 August 1938 car 112 is being chased by an intended passenger as it moves off on the 85 route to Spon Lane, West Smethwick. Within a year this UEC-built tram-car of 1906 had been broken up at West Smethwick depot by John Cashmore Ltd of Great Bridge. The second tram is 130, another of the 71 Class cars, on the 29 route to Bearwood, while beneath the stone arch of the bridge is car 256, one of the ex-open-topped, three-bay-construction Brill 21E-truck cars that had been fitted with a bow collector for working on the Lodge Road route. *W. A. Camwell*

Car 206 had just started to leave the terminus beneath the Council House extension bridge in Edmund Street. It is in service on the short-working 30 route to Windmill Lane, Smethwick, during 1938. The 1907-built, open-balconied four-wheeler is carrying a fairly unusual advertisement for Symington's Coffee Essence. Behind it is bogie car 743, one of Rosebery Street depot's Brush-built, 63 hp, EMB air-brake trams, which is being employed on the 55 route. This was also a short-working of the main line, going only as far as Grove Lane at the city boundary. *R. T. Wilson*

Car 74 is leaving Edmund Street on route W, which was later to be numbered 30, and is about to turn into Congreve Street. The tram is in its original condition with open-vestibuled platforms and balconies. It carries the flop-over destination canopy boards for 'EDMUND ST TO WINDMILL LANE', while on the side it also carries a slipboard for Windmill Lane. Just visible in the gloom of the arched bridge is a horse-drawn tower-wagon.

The photograph was taken in about 1912 as the Council House extension had been completed that June after a construction period of over two years. The tram is in the middle of the road, which further helps to date this view, as kerb-side loading in Edmund Street was not introduced until late 1913. On the base plinth of the Council House, where the lamp-post in the foreground is casting its shadow, is an official Ordnance Survey benchmark, while on the balustrade, a few feet away, a wag has drawn in chalk a couple of wine glasses. *T. Lewis*

On leaving Congreve Street the trams descended the steep hill of Summer Row and crossed the Birmingham & Fazeley Canal by Saturday Bridge, allegedly so called because of the canal boatmen who waited to be paid there every Saturday. The bridge is visible just behind the distant tram towards the top of the hill. Car 196 crosses the junction on Wednesday 12 April 1939 and passes the early Victorian factory, at 66 Parade, of paint manufacturers Hoyle, Robson Barnett & Co Ltd. The tram is on the service to St Paul's Road, Smethwick. The track in the foreground to the left will take the distant tram, number 53, into the Jewellery Quarter by way of Newhall Hill. Car 53 was one of the small UEC-built 48-seaters fitted with bow collectors for the 32 service along Lodge Road. *H. B. Priestley*

Car 191 is in the Parade, about half a mile from the edge of Birmingham city centre. It is coming into the city from Bearwood on Sunday 13 June 1937 and is passing George Mason's grocery shop, which was located between Camden Street and George Street. George Mason was a large West Bromwich-based grocery chain well-known until competition from the large supermarket stores. Car 191 entered service in December 1906 and spent most of its life allocated to Rosebery Street depot, being withdrawn in September 1939. *A. D. Packer*

Car 181 loads at the Bulpitts hollow-ware factory, about 100 yards on the city side of the Monument Road/Icknield Street junction, in Summer Hill Road on 24 March 1939. This 52-seat tram, which is working into the city, was built by UEC in 1906, and was unique in its class by having side-window ventilators to the upper saloon. This experimental top-cover, a prototype for the 301 Class, had originally been fitted to car 104, and was subsequently removed from that tram when it was converted to open-top in 1917. Car 181 had been re-trucked with a Brush-Peckham P35 truck, which with vestibuling and re-seating had increased the weight of the cars from 11 tons 17 cwt to 12 tons 3 cwt 2 qtr. These 71 Class cars could be distinguished from the later 301 Class, not only by their increased height, but also by having round dash-panels and a deeper platform window, which omitted the signal light above it. In the foreground the wide space between the two tracks is a relic of when the line had originally been wired with centre poles, which was a very rare feature on the BCT system. *L. W. Perkins*

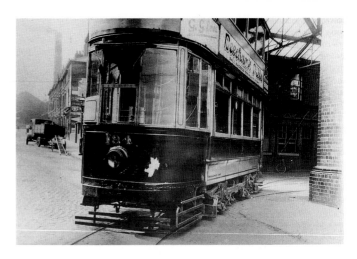

Left Access to Rosebery Street depot from the main-line routes in Spring Hill was by way of College Street. This cobbled street was lined with a mixture of mid-19th-century terraces and the slightly earlier courtyards, including the oddly named Alma Mater.

Car 747, one of the depot's 11 Brush-bodied air-brake bogie trams at this time, travels away from the depot in 1947, the last year of tramcar operation from Rosebery Street, to take up duty on the Ladywood route. *J. S. Webb*

Above Rosebery Street depot was opened on 14 April 1906 and initially operated the Lodge Road service; after 1 July the Bearwood and Soho services were also introduced from the depot. Subsequently the Hagley Road and Ladywood routes were also operated, resulting in an allocation of about 75 trams being housed here.

This unusual view, albeit with part of the tram's upper saloon missing from the photograph, shows some minor accident damage to the dash-panel of ex-Radial car 194. The tram is standing at the entrance to the depot on Tuesday 1 May 1928. Further up Rosebery Street the solid-tyred lorry with the open cab is parked with its wheels against the kerb, so that it will not roll backwards. *D. Sanders collection*

Left As late as 1938 Rosebery Street depot could boast of having 35 cars of the 71 Class to operate on the main Dudley Road routes, 17 of the small Brill-type to work on the twisty Lodge Road route and about 15 bogie cars, mainly from the air-braked 732 Class, to be used on the 33 route to nearby Ladywood and for short-workings to Grove Lane and Windmill Lane.

This 1938 line-up of 71 Class ex-Radial trams has on the left car 128, which was withdrawn after being the last service car into Hockley depot in the early hours of Sunday 2 April 1939. The remaining three cars, 207, 181 and 76, would all be withdrawn between May and September 1939. Car 207 would survive the war, having been kept in store at Rosebery Street as a reserve car, although like all the other stored tramcars of the 71 Class, it was never used. *W. A. Camwell*

Left Car 180 is being delayed by the overhead repair crew, who are making some wiring adjustments, on top of their Tilling-Stevens tower-wagon No 7 (O 9922). This is waiting in Dudley Road at the Soho Loop canal bridge on Thursday 6 October 1932 when working on the 29 route to Bearwood.

The Soho Loop canal had originally been the main line, but had been replaced in 1829 when Thomas Telford's new 453-foot summit line was opened between Birmingham and Wolverhampton, which reduced the distance between the two towns by a third. The Soho Loop only exists today because factories that pre-dated the Telford main line were replaced by industrial premises on the same site, which continued to use the canal for transport access and also as a source for water. It was at the Winson Green Prison end of the Soho Loop that infamously, on 12 August 1964, one of the Great Train Robbers escaped along the tow-path. *D. R. Harvey collection*

Right On Tuesday 27 September 1939 tramcars 193, from West Smethwick depot working on the 85 route to Spon Lane, and similar 71 Class car 124 allocated to Rosebery Street depot, pass on Lee Bridge, Dudley Road. In the foreground is the curve that car 124, working the 31 service, has used to turn left out of Heath Street. Lee Bridge crossed the straightened Birmingham & Wolverhampton Canal that had been rebuilt by Thomas Telford, as well as the former LNWR Stour Valley railway line. In the background is St Patrick's Roman Catholic church. *W. A. Camwell*

Soho branch

Right The 31 route was the most infrequent route operated by Birmingham's trams, requiring only two cars to maintain the off-peak service. The 1¼-mile branch ran along Heath Street, which had been built from the 1830s over part of an infertile tract of land known as Birmingham Heath.

On Wednesday 7 September 1938 ex-Radial car 159 turns in front of the Lee Bridge Tavern on its way towards Soho. It is being followed by a 1932 panel van belonging to tinware manufacturers Thomas Cowley, while the AOC-registered van that is astride the out-of-town tram tracks belongs to Guest, Keen & Nettlefold, of Heath Street, famous for screw manufacturing. This company had been set up in 1854 by the Nettlefold and Chamberlain families; one of the partners was Joseph Chamberlain, whose Liberal paternalism helped transform his adopted town into one of the best-run cities in the country. *W. A. Camwell*

Below right Permanent Way car PW 9 poses in Heath Street on 4 April 1938, in front of the three-storeyed terraces and courts that lined the road from the Dudley Road junction as far as the Birmingham boundary. It is interesting to see that the houses in the distance, nearest to Dudley Road, were built with bands of lighter brickwork, while the slightly later terraces behind the tram are built to a simpler and therefore cheaper specification.

PW 9 had the body of ex-CBT car 509, which had been built by the Electric Railway & Tramway Carriage Works Ltd (ER&TCW) in 1901 for the newly electrified Bristol Road service. Car 509 was one of two four-wheel trams to be converted to single-deck trailers; the other was car 28, which apparently never worked in that state. In the autumn of 1928 the body of car 509 was mounted on the Conaty truck of a similar car, the former 507, which had served as the original PW 9 since 1921. This hybrid vehicle was to remain in service until March 1952, being one of the only two Permanent Way cars to receive the post-war blue and cream livery instead of the all-over blue seen here. *H. B. Priestley*

On the last day of operation, 30 September 1939, car 73 stands in Cranford Street when working the 31 service. It is approaching Soho Street and is about to turn right to the terminus on the bridge at the railway station. The Bon Cafe is still able to do bacon and eggs for 6d, so wartime restrictions had obviously not yet bitten. To the left is the Old Crystal Palace public house, which supplied M&B beer from the nearby Cape Hill brewery. With the war nearly a month old, all the street furniture has been given its white markings, but this 71 Class tram, on its last day in service, as it would be sent to Rosebery Street for storage until 1945, has not been fitted with a headlight mask and has only its fender painted white. *R. T. Coxon*

Soho station was on the former LNWR main line between Birmingham and Wolverhampton, and the 31 tram terminus was on the railway bridge in Soho Street near its junction with Rabone Lane. Car 75 stands at the terminus while its crew pose for the photographer. It is Tuesday 2 August 1938 and at the Birmingham Hippodrome the Radio Rodeo bill seems fairly uninspiring with only the singer Billy Scott-Coomber being well-known. *W. A. Camwell*

The comparison between the 1938 view of car 75 and that taken in August 1994 reveals an almost unrecognisable scene. The parapet of the bridge to the left is all that remains from pre-war days. The station closed on 23 May 1949 and all the Victorian houses were demolished by the early '60s, to be replaced by the flats in the distance, which are in Windmill Lane. Oddly enough the view to right and left along Rabone Lane has hardly changed in the intervening years. *D. R. Harvey*

Ladywood and Cape Hill

For barely six months, 301 Class cars were drafted into Rosebery Street to replace the older 71 Class cars, which had generally gone to West Smethwick depot for scrapping. Some 22 of the 301 cars arrived from Selly Oak, replaced by bogie cars from the recent Hockley abandonment. Here car 306 stands at the Heath Street junction outside the Lee Bridge Tavern on a sunny day in the summer of 1939. In the background, across the road from the trees that hide Dudley Road Hospital, is the tall nave of the architecturally uninspired St Patrick's Roman Catholic Church. *Newman College*

Dudley Road in 1993 had become a much busier road and very little of the 1939 scene remained. With 29 as the service number, the preserved 1950 ex-BCT Crossley 2489 (JOJ 489) stands opposite where tram 306 unloaded its two passengers. The Lee Bridge Tavern, on the corner of Heath Street, remains, but the shops on the opposite corner have been demolished and replaced by an advertising hoarding. Just above this can be seen some of the 1960s extensions to Dudley Road Hospital. Turning into Heath Street on the 443 route is a Midland Red West Leyland 'Lynx', which entered service in 1989. *D. R. Harvey*

As the Commer 1-ton lorry speeds by, a woman with two children, one in a pram and an older girl with her fairy cycle, shields her eyes from the late afternoon sun as she waits for an opportunity to cross Dudley Road. It is Wednesday 12 April 1939, and former Radial car 102, working to Dudley on the 87 service, is picking up passengers at the compulsory stop outside McKies' Bargain Store.

The tram tracks curving to the right led into Icknield Port Road and were only used by depot workings from Rosebery Street to gain access to the Ladywood, 33, route, whose terminus was just around the corner. The busy street scene beyond the tram is virtually unaltered today, although where the woman with the pram is standing is now the site of the realigned Winson Green Road. The distant roof of St Patrick's church is visible above the small Atkinsons brewery lorry. *H. B. Priestley*

The Ladywood route was looked at in Volume 1, but the proximity of its terminus to the Dudley Road services is worth repeating in order to place it in its geographical context.

Car 732, the first of 30 Brush-bodied, EMB air-brake cars of 1926, stands opposite the Bundy Clock at the terminus of the 33 route on 23 March 1946. The Dudley Road shops, where the woman and children of the previous picture were standing, can be seen in the background. *Burrows Bros*

Returning to Dudley Road, its routes were operated from Rosebery Street garage until it was closed on 29 June 1968. The second generation of buses to operate on these routes were 2196-2230, which were the last 35 of the 2181 Class of Park Royal-bodied Leyland 'Titan' PD2/1s. 2223 (JOJ 223) is passing Summerfield Park in Dudley Road in about 1959 on the B82 service to Bearwood, direct successor to the 29 tram route.

The former Black Country tram routes often gave the impression that they were not really part of the rest of the Birmingham bus system. This was perpetuated almost to the end of Corporation bus operation, as these attractive yet totally non-standard buses, with their 'B'-prefixed destination blinds, were the backbone of the Dudley Road services for nearly all their lives. *A. B. Cross*

On the right a Vulcan-bodied AEC 'Regent' is being overtaken by an Austin car while loading up in City Road, Edgbaston, when working on the 11 route. Meanwhile, in the distance on Dudley Road ex-Radial car 119, one of West Smethwick's 45-strong allocation of 71 Class cars, works towards Smethwick on the short-working 80 route to St Paul's Road. It is standing by the trees that mark the edge of Summerfield Park, a lung of greenery amidst the Victorian development that had been built all the way to the city boundary at Grove Lane. The 12-acre park had been opened in 1878 on the site of the late Lucas Chance's Summerfield House and grounds. By 1937, when this photograph was taken, the park covered a rhomboid-shaped area of 34 acres. *Commercial postcard*

Above The Grove Cinema had only been open for six years when, on 12 April 1939, George Formby's latest film *It's In The Air* was showing. The cinema stood at the bottom of Dudley Road next to the Cape of Good Hope public house at Grove Lane, and was to remain until 1981 when it was closed and eventually converted into a shop.

Tramcar 93 is working towards Birmingham from Dudley and as it approaches the cross-over used by the 55 route trams working only to Grove Lane it leaves the ice-cream seller and his handcart in shadow as it comes to a halt at the Birmingham-Smethwick boundary stop outside the cinema. *H. B. Priestley*

Below Looking in the other direction towards Cape Hill, standing opposite the Cape of Good Hope public house is car 124, having worked the 55 route to Grove Lane. It has had its trolley-pole reversed prior to returning to Edmund Street via the cross-over, much to the chagrin of the queuing passengers. The tramcar is still operating from Rosebery Street in this 1938 view, but would be transferred to West Smethwick depot in early May 1939 for the last five months of the Dudley via Smethwick route.

Off the picture to the left and opposite the three-storeyed houses in the distance is the Mitchells & Butlers Cape Hill Brewery, which brewed its first beer in July 1879 and is still the centre of M&B operations. *W. A. Camwell*

Left Climbing up Cape Hill towards Windmill Lane is Birmingham & Midland Tramways car 20. This tram, built by the Brush Company in 1904, belonged to the series of trams that were used by most of the Black Country tramway companies, known as the 'Aston' type. It was mounted on a Brush-built Lycett & Conaty 8 ft 6 in radial truck and seated 48 passengers. It is passing the school on the corner of Durban Road; having just passed the Cape Hill brewery, it carries an appropriate Mitchells & Butler advertisement below the open balcony. *D. R. Harvey collection*

Middle left On 23 September 1939 car 310 approaches the crest of the steep descent in Cape Hill and passes the Cape Cycle Co on its way towards the city. This 301 Class car had been transferred to Rosebery Street depot from Selly Oak in June 1939, and on the closure of the routes through Smethwick would eventually reappear in May 1940 at Coventry Road depot on the Stechford services. Due for withdrawal in 1940, it would remain in service until 2 October 1949. *J. S. Webb*

Below left The area around Cape Hill at the Windmill Lane junction was developed as a shopping centre at the turn of the century. The large gabled premises to the right still stand today; they were occupied by the purveyors of grocery and provisions, the Universal Tea Company, and stand on the corner of Windmill Lane, having replaced a post office, which had been on the site since the middle of the 19th century.

To the left is the turn into Waterloo Road, and here is the first clue to the date of the photograph; there are tram tracks laid into that road, and the Birmingham & Midland Tramways Company opened this service on 24 November 1904. The large house behind the trees between Waterloo Road and the High Street was called The Elms and was demolished in about 1906 to make way for the Lloyds Bank building that still occupies the site.

The two tramcars are standing at the B&M's short-working terminus at Windmill Lane. The tram to the left is B&M car 4, a Brush-built car of October 1904, running on Brush AA-type rigid trucks. It has been fitted with a Dick, Kerr 'Bellamy'-style short, uncanopied top-cover. The open-top car to the right appears to be carrying the number 211 or 213, which means that it is a City of Birmingham Tramways Company tramcar. It was delivered in November 1904 and was presumably on loan to the Birmingham & Midland when new. From this detective work it must be assumed that this view was taken within weeks of the opening of the electric tram services to Smethwick. Ah! But the leaves on the trees would mean that it wasn't November. However, on another copy the leaves are not there - they were painted on the postcard! *Commercial postcard*

Cape Hill, Smethwick.

Right In about 1927 rebuilt ex-CBT tramcar 460 emerges from Waterloo Road on the 29 route on its way to the city. The Elms has long since given way to Lloyds Bank, while a plethora of attic gables stretches away on both sides of the bank towards Bearwood and Smethwick. Brush-built car 460 of 1904 had been numbered 200 by CBT, and when taken over had been the only one of the 193-208 series remaining in the earlier Munich lake and cream livery. After rebuilding with a top-cover and vestibuled platforms, the tram ran until March 1938 when it was withdrawn. Obscured by the cyclist on the right in High Street is a 71 Class car about to cross over and return to the city. Beyond that is Birmingham & Midland company car 16, which is working towards Smethwick. *D. R. Harvey collection*

Below Cape Hill was a busy suburban shopping centre and was a hive of activity in this view from about 1937, looking from the Lloyds Bank building. To the left, on the corner of Windmill Lane, is a George Mason grocery shop, replacing the earlier Universal Tea Company, while next door, originating from the same town, is the West Bromwich Building Society. Opposite and slightly obscured by the ornate lamp-standard in the foreground, is the Seven Stars Hotel; today it is known as the Seven Stars public house. On the right of the junction, on the corner of Shireland Road, is the well-known Birmingham-based pork butchers, Marsh & Baxter.

Car 136 will continue straight on as it travels on its way to Dudley on the 87 route. It will pass the policeman on point duty who is wearing a cap that is of a different design to those worn by police in Birmingham. The tracks in the right foreground take the 29 tram service to Bearwood. *Commercial postcard*

Bearwood

Above Standing at the traffic lights in Waterloo Road on 6 January 1938 is car 130. It is on the Bearwood route and is about to join the main line at the Cape Hill junction. To the left is the Edwardian-built Lloyds Bank, while opposite can be seen both the Seven Stars Hotel and, to the left of Windmill Lane, the local branch of George Mason, advertising itself as 'Cash Grocer' on the awning.

Following the tram is a 1935 Austin Ten-Four saloon and a large, unidentified Smethwick-registered saloon. Car 130 would be one of the casualties of the Hockley closure, as it would be withdrawn from Rosebery Street in April 1939 on being replaced by 301 Class cars, of which some 22 would be in service at that depot by June 1939. *H. B. Priestley*

Below In Bearwood Road the trams had to pass along a section of inter-laced track between Ethel Street and Sandon Road, about half a mile from the Bearwood terminus. On 29 July 1939 UEC-bodied, four-wheel car 306 of April 1911 loads up outside the bakers near the corner of Three Shires Oak Road. The large domed building above and behind the tram is the Bear Hotel, an Ansells pub that still dominates the junction today. *H. B. Priestley*

The junction on the left is Three Shires Oak Road, which commemorates the Three Shires Oak that marked the one-time boundary of Staffordshire with detached parts of Worcestershire and Shropshire. The oak tree was felled in 1904, only months before the opening of the Bearwood tram route by the Birmingham & Midland Tramway Company on 24 November 1904. The Bear Inn casts a long afternoon shadow across the junction where the tram tracks go from interlaced to double line. Car 177 stands on this interlaced section as it waits at the stop outside the bakers before continuing to Birmingham on the 29 route. The distant tower is Bearwood Road school. The shops clustered around Sandon Road to the right appear to belong to a much more confident period of development at the end of the Victorian period and contained in this mid-1920s view a George Mason grocers as well as a chemist. *Commercial postcard*

Bearwood Road in about 1910 or earlier was lined on both sides mainly with houses, with the exception of the public house on the corner of Poplar Road, which sold Cheshires Ales whose brewery was in Windmill Lane, and a few shops just beyond the tram, which have been converted to retail premises. Car 203, with open platforms and balconies, has left the Bearwood terminus; it carries a letter 'B' stencil on a black background to denote that it is on the BEAR-WOOD TO EDMUND ST service, which was displayed on the flop-over boards. *Commercial postcard*

The Bearwood terminus was outside Wrensons grocers in Bearwood Road, one of the shops in the same buildings that appear in the previous photograph as houses. Until 1930 there was only a few yards distance between this terminus and that of the 34 route at the Kings Head public house (see page 13). Car 89 stands a few yards from the terminal stub next to the Bundy Clock in the summer of 1939.

This tram, fitted with a Brush 8 ft 6 in truck in 1914 to replace the original unsuccessful Mountain & Gibson Radial truck, was to see service until the closure of the Smethwick routes at the end of September 1939, and became one of the 22 cars of the 71 Class that were retained in store in case of wartime emergencies. *W. A. Camwell*

Cape Hill to Smethwick

Back at Cape Hill, in High Street on the west side of Cape Hill junction, is UEC-bodied ex-Radial car 215, which has just crossed over and is waiting to return to the city on service 30. Just visible on the other side of the junction are trams coming from Birmingham, which have arrived at this important shopping centre. Car 215 had been transferred from West Smethwick depot in 1929. It was to remain at Rosebery Street depot until April 1939 when it was withdrawn. *W. A. Camwell*

The steam tram tracks were doubled between the Birmingham boundary and the Windmill Lane coke yard just on the Smethwick side of Cape Hill junction by 1898. The driver and the cigarette-smoking conductor stand alongside their respective charges. The steam locomotive is an 1886-built Kitson, which is running firebox first, with the chimney nearest to the trailer. This was the more common way round to run the combination, if routes had turning loops or tri-angles, although the CBT steam trams generally ran chimney first. In this case there was origi-nally no such option as the Lionel Street termi-nus in Birmingham had no such facility to reverse the tram until a reversing triangle was installed about 1888. The trailer is one of six cars numbered 17-22 that were built by Starbuck, also in 1886, although it appears to be numbered 13 in this turn of the century view. The tram and trailer are well covered with adver-tisements, with only McDougalls self-raising flour being a non-household cleaning product. *Dr H. A. Whitcombe*

The 1936-registered Armstrong-Siddeley Twelve-Plus, parked opposite Smethwick Council House, was priced when new at £320, which was about three-quarters of the cost of a new semi-detached house in the suburbs of Birmingham. On the far side of High Street are the gates of Victoria Park, opened in 1888 and occupying 35 acres of land in the heart of Smethwick. Its cottage-style gatehouse reflects the architectural style of the Arts and Crafts movement that was considered appropriate for parks towards the end of the last century.

It is Wednesday 12 April 1939 and West Smethwick-allocated car 88, one of 45 cars of the 71 Class assigned to that depot, has come down the hill from Cape Hill junction on service 87 to Dudley. *H. B. Priestley*

BIRMINGHAM TRAMS 1933-53

The George Inn stood on the north side of High Street at the corner of Brasshouse Lane, but was demolished in 1981 to make way for Tollhouse Way, built to bypass High Street. Car 159 has arrived from Birmingham on the 86 route. It is September 1939 and the wartime white road markings on kerbs and street furniture have been painted in order to help pedestrians and traffic during hours of darkness. The tram has also had its fender painted white. The trams used for the Dudley routes were placed in store for a short time after the closure, in case the routes might be reinstated. The local authorities outside the city would not agree to the cost of track relaying even in wartime, which in hindsight appears to have been a convenient excuse, and car 159 along with the other 49 of the Class that ended up at West Smethwick, was broken up by Cashmores of Great Bridge. *Newman College*

One of the Birmingham & Midland Aston-type top-covered cars of 1904, in this case perhaps car 48, travels along High Street on its way to Oldbury in about 1913. It has just passed the reading library and the Blue Gates Hotel, whose sign can be seen near the large lanterned street light on the corner of Stony Lane. All the buildings on this side of the High Street are still occupied, although today the other side of the road is now an open space to Tollhouse Way.

There has recently been a heavy rainstorm that has left the pavements very wet, but even more noticeably the mud on the road is more reminiscent of a cowboy town in the American Mid-West than Smethwick! *P. Jaques collection*

High Street, Smethwick, was a bustling shopping centre that gradually declined in importance after the Second World War and was finally emasculated by having one side of it removed! In this scene there are numerous delivery lorries unloading, including the coal merchant's small vehicle. People are going about their business apart from the man just to the rear of the tram who appears to be taking up a pose for the benefit of the photographer.

Car 131 has worked into Smethwick from Oldbury on the 86 service on Thursday 14 April 1938, and is at the western end of the High Street at its junction with St Paul's Road. Tollhouse Way now separates the High Street from the railway line. Where the tram is standing is today a wide grassy bank and a children's play area. *H. B. Priestley*

West Smethwick and Oldbury

There were only four places on the Birmingham tram system where operation was controlled by signal lights, and three of them were on the Oldbury route. At Oldbury Road near Smethwick Junction station, the road narrowed over the former GWR's Stourbridge Extension line, which meant that the track was interlaced over the bridge; the controlling traffic light for the westbound trams to Dudley can be seen on the nearest traction pole.

Car 129 is travelling towards Smethwick in the early part of 1939 and has just passed the garage premises of Roebuck Engineering, on the corner of Roebuck Lane. The tram is working on the 86 service, which was a West Smethwick duty, and had been allocated to that depot since its transfer from Coventry Road/Arthur Street in July 1928. It would remain there until the Dudley routes closed. *J. S. Webb*

Car 185 works along the interlaced track towards Oldbury on Wednesday 23 August 1939. It is being followed by a three-wheel delivery van that appears to be a James Handyvan, which was manufactured in Greet, Birmingham. Behind the petrol station in Roebuck Lane is Galton Bridge, which crossed railway and canal in one magnificent 150-foot cast-iron span bridge. Designed by Thomas Telford and opened in 1828, it is one of the gems of the Industrial Revolution. The bridge survives today and is restored to its original condition, but has been replaced for motor traffic by Telford Way, which is by contrast an uninspired concrete viaduct. *W. A. Camwell*

Above Open balcony car 84 travels along Oldbury Road, West Smethwick, at Hawthorn Street, which is to the left of the photograph and near Spon Lane; it is passing Oldbury Road School on the 86 service to Oldbury on Wednesday 12 April 1939. Approaching the tram on a road surface of stone setts by the tramlines and tarmac on either side, is a brand new Fordson E83W 10 cwt van on West Bromwich trade plates, and the tram is being followed by an equally new Morris Eight. All of this area has been swept away except for a few shops that are masked by the tram. Car 84 was to remain in service until the final day of tramcar operation in the Black Country and was eventually broken up in the spring of 1940. *H. B. Priestley*

Right The section of line from St Paul's Road to Oldbury went along Oldbury Road, passing the junction at the Spon Croft public house, which until November 1929 was on the Birmingham & District single-deck tram route from West Bromwich. Beyond the Spon Lane junction was West Smethwick depot, whose curved entrance tracks can be seen in the foreground. The depot had been used by BCT from 1 April 1928 along with the 6.17 route miles from Grove Lane to Dudley.

Car 148, on its way from Dudley to Smethwick on an 87 service, has stopped at the CARS STOP HERE IF REQUIRED stop, mounted on the traction pole to the extreme left, to pick up workmen. It is Thursday 14 April 1938 and UEC-bodied car 148 would run for another 13 months before being withdrawn as 301 Class cars were drafted in to work on the services operated by Rosebery Street depot. *H. B. Priestley*

Looking in the opposite direction from the previous photograph, this view shows more clearly that the bus stop plate is already in position outside the entrance to West Smethwick depot on the final day of operation of trams on the Smethwick, Oldbury and Dudley service. This was the last group of tram services in the Black Country to remain in operation. These routes had survived, along with the West Bromwich, Wednesbury and Dudley services, also operated by BCT, as the remnants of a once large narrow-gauge tram system, the rest having finally succumbed to the bus some nine years before. Car 108, by now 33 years old, stands on the depot entrance triangle tracks on its way towards Oldbury and Dudley on service 87. Only the row of houses in the distance remain today with the M5 elevated motorway dominating the skyline above those terraces. *R. T. Coxon*

With just over one week left of operation on the Dudley route, car 107 stands with the gloomy sheds of West Smethwick depot looming behind it on Friday 23 September 1939. The 71 Class trams had been used on the routes taken over from the Birmingham & District Company on 1 April 1928. The Corporation was very short of trams at this time and although it had ordered 50 bogie cars, it had to hire all the 38 trams allocated by the Company to West Smethwick depot in order to maintain the services. Gradually, during the next few months, the Corporation managed to get enough cars together so that the Company trams could be returned, mainly for scrap, and the ex-Radial cars were drafted in to monopolise these acquired Black Country services until abandonment in 1939. *J. S. Webb*

All the West Smethwick tramcar allocation in service at the closure of the Dudley and Smethwick routes was stored at that depot in case the route was to be reinstated. The decision to scrap the 71 Class cars was taken by December 1939 and they were sold to Cashmores of Great Bridge. However, the lower saloon of at least two cars escaped this fate. The remains of the other car, 147, can be seen on page 19 of Volume 1, while car 107 found itself being used as a summer house in Charford near Bromsgrove. Seen here on 1 April 1988, it was acquired for preservation and can now be seen in the Aston Manor Transport Museum, which is located at the old Witton depot. *D. R. Harvey*

West Smethwick depot was opened by the Birmingham & Midland Tramways Company in the summer of 1885 on a 3½-acre site, and operated steam trams until converted for electric tramcars in November 1904. It had three gable-ended sheds with 11 roads leading off a narrow single entrance in Oldbury Road. The Tat Bank branch of the Titford Canal ran behind where the photographer was standing, and between canal and car sheds were, in later days, two quite long sidings.

This view of the depot yard taken on 9 March 1939 shows two identifiable members of the 71 Class in the depot, cars 186 and 208, but in the foreground is car 335. This former Selly Oak tram had been taken out of service on 9 November 1938 after some collision damage to the platform and was one of only two 301 Class cars to be broken up at West Smethwick. Close examination reveals that the route number box and the upper saloon glass have already been removed. *D. R. Harvey collection*

The scrapping of redundant trams continued throughout the 1930s, and after 1937 the four-wheel cars inherited from the City of Birmingham Tramways Company were quickly withdrawn because they were non-standard and not required for further service. Car 474, formerly CBT car 182, built by Brush in 1903, originally with Brush equal-wheel D-type bogies, is parked on the line adjacent to the Tat Bank canal in May 1938 awaiting breaking up. This was the only member of the eight cars of the Class taken over by the Corporation in July 1911 to be equipped with the quieter helical gears. Behind it is car 456, a 48-seater tram built by the Brush Company in 1904, which had originally been CBT's 196. As with the 71 Class cars, these ex-Company cars had been an obvious choice for early withdrawal because of their DK6A 35 hp motors, their high-bridge construction and lack of upholstered seating. *W. A. Camwell*

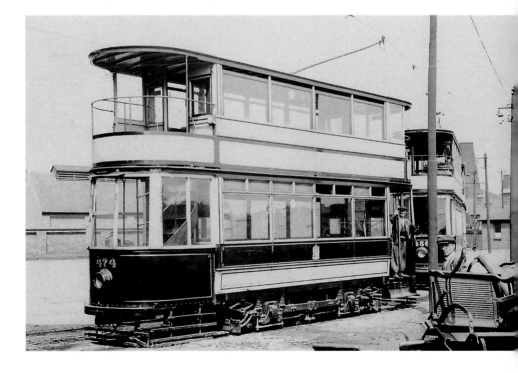

The main A457 road entered Oldbury via Birmingham Street. On the last day of operation, 30 September 1939, a busy Saturday shopping day, car 124 passes Church Square, which has a branch of Barclays Bank on the corner. The tram is in service on the 87 route and is travelling towards Dudley. It will be using the bus stop which, unlike the gas-light just behind the gasmask-carrying cyclists, has yet to be painted with wartime white stripes. The iron railings on the right stand in front of Christ Church, the rather severe parish church built in 1840; the railings were lost the following year in the wartime scrap metal drive. *R. T. Coxon*

Towards the Market Place end of Birmingham Street, the road became much narrower and the tram tracks had to be laid very close together. This meant that the section of the route from the Market Place to Unity Place, where the lorry is unloading, just in front of the Old Cross, although double-track, was operated as a single-line section because trams were unable to pass. This section was controlled by coloured signal lights, which were operated by actuators on the overhead. Car 178 is about halfway along this section of Birmingham Street and is approaching its 86 route terminus in Oldbury on 23 August 1939. *W. A. Camwell*

Birmingham Street has changed very little since the trams departed in 1939. While the buildings on the left have been replaced, the rest of the street has managed to escape the redevelopment that has totally altered the Market Place, which is now dominated by the Sava Centre supermarket. The Junction public house now occupies the Victorian building on the corner of Unity Place and Birmingham Street and the road itself remains very much as it did when 71 Class trams echoed between the narrow buildings. *D. R. Harvey*

BIRMINGHAM TRAMS 1933-53

Above The coronation of George VI took place in May 1937 and many places, including Oldbury, put up bunting and flags to celebrate the event. Car 80 travels across the open space of the Market Place on its way towards the narrow entrance into Birmingham Street. Standing in the square is a Midland Red Brush-bodied FEDD-type double-decker in its smartly lined-out livery. To the left of the view is Church Street, which leads to Bromford Lane. This had been served until 1929 by a single-deck tram route operated by the Birmingham & District Company, the curve of the setts still marking the line of this abandoned route. *W. A. Camwell*

Below Seen in 1995 from the same position as the previous photograph, the buildings on the corner of Birmingham Street and Halesowen Street have survived intact despite the wholesale redevelopment of the bus station to accommodate the Sava Centre shopping centre. The new buildings on the corner of Church Street were erected after the site had remained derelict for many years and are of an architectural style and scale that fits in with the older shops in Oldbury. *D. R. Harvey*

On to Dudley

Former Radial car 92 is about to enter a passing loop near Brades Locks on Dudley Road East. The surrounding waste ground west of Oldbury had been derelict for many years and bore testimony to the decline in heavy industry in the Black Country caused by the exhaustion of the locally extracted raw materials.

Car 92, seen on 23 September 1939, is working on the 87 service and, like the street furniture, has had its fender painted white as part of the wartime measures to make it more visible in the blackout. This West Smethwick-based tram remained in service until the route closure eight days later, and would be dismantled by Cashmores in April 1940. *J. S. Webb*

The Boat Inn marked the junction of Dudley Road East and Tipton Road, and it was here that the trams passed on to another section of single-line track that was controlled by traffic signals for the trams. This was because the main road towards Tividale and Burnt Tree climbed sharply over the bridge of the Birmingham Canal Navigation's Old Main Line. Car 196, even at this late stage of its career able to reflect in its excellent paintwork the light-coloured dress of the woman alighting from it, is seen on 23 August 1939 working the 87 route on its way to Dudley. *W. A. Camwell*

At the Boat public house in 1993 very little remains from the 1939 view. All the early-19th-century cottages and the original Boat Inn were demolished by the 1960s to be replaced by a housing estate and the architecturally anonymous Banks's hostelry. The canal bridge remains a hump-back on Dudley Road West, and traffic crossing into Tipton Road, as the Bedford TK lorry is doing here, has to exercise a good deal of caution when negotiating the junction. *D. R. Harvey*

BIRMINGHAM TRAMS 1933-53

Above Car 107 again! On 12 April 1939 it is seen at the entrance tracks to the former Birmingham & Midland Tividale tram depot and works, when working on the 87 route to Dudley. Today all the Victorian terraced housing has been replaced by a large development of 'starter homes'. Tividale Works opened on 1 January 1907 and finally closed down in March 1930, but the track and the overhead remained in situ for feeder purposes from the sub-station in the depot yard until the end of tramcar operation on the route. *H. B. Priestley*

Below Travelling away from Dudley towards Oldbury is car 84. It too is opposite the entrance of Tividale Works, which is marked by the long disused triangle of the entrance track. On Thursday 6 January 1938 the tram has just cleared Tividale Street, to the left, and is being approached by a large Birmingham-registered saloon. This section of track had deteriorated considerably during the 1930s and the 71 Class cars, with their hard riding characteristics and wooden seats, were uncomfortable enough without this added difficulty.

The 87 route was always operated by four-wheel trams, yet on an enthusiasts' tour in 1938 lightweight car 843 reached Dudley for the second time in that year. This time, however, it returned to Birmingham via Oldbury and Smethwick! The only other time Birmingham bogie cars used the route was after the West Bromwich closure in April 1939, when some of Hockley depot's trams were transferred to other depots by way of this route. *H. B. Priestley*

Above At Burnt Tree, the 87 route joined the 74 service from West Bromwich. A Birmingham-bound tram on the 87 route is crossing the tracks for the West Bromwich route in Birmingham Road. Just visible above the roof of the Morris Y series 10 cwt van on the left is one of the West Bromwich Corporation Daimler COG6 double-deck buses. The tram has passed a Morrison battery-electric milk float and has driven in front of the Fordson 7V series lorry that is travelling towards Dudley.

The scene is still recognisable today. The road is a dual-carriageway, but still has the same alignment, while the houses to the left were only demolished in about 1991 to make way for a large Tesco supermarket. *D. R. Harvey collection*

Below Car 98 stands opposite the Midland Red bus garage on Sunday 23 October 1938 on the occasion when Birmingham's last tramcar, 843, was used by the LRTL to travel from Dudley to Rednal. The 1906 vintage 71 Class trams were built without vestibules and could always be recognised by their slightly sloping enclosed platform windows after rebuilding.

The tram has just arrived from Oldbury and the driver on the pavement on the extreme left must be wondering why crowds of people are gathering around the distant modern-looking car 843 parked at the terminus about 100 yards away. *A. N. H. Glover*

The terminus for both Birmingham Corporation routes was on the railway bridge above Dudley station, although there had been a request in 1928 by Dudley Council that the terminus be moved to the top of Castle Hill; this was rejected as it was alleged that the Board of Trade would not allow closed-top, narrow-gauge trams up and down such a steep hill. Car 80 on the 87 route stands in front of a Hockley depot bogie car on the 74 service in February 1939. Both trams have had their poles turned before returning to Birmingham by their respective routes.

In the background is the Midland Red's Dudley garage with an SOS FEDD double-decker parked outside. The garage was opened on 2 August 1929, and was taken over by the West Midland Passenger Transport Executive on 3 December 1973; closed in September 1993, it was finally demolished in 1994 to make way for a ring road around Dudley town centre. *J. S. Webb*

On 23 October 1938 the LRTL hired Birmingham's newest tram, 843, to undertake what was regarded as something of an epic tour of the system. It was organised by the late Arthur Camwell and took the enthusiasts from Dudley to Rednal. The modern lines of the tram are a contrast to the elderly 71 Class cars coming in from Oldbury on the 87 service, and although on this trip 843 went back again via Great Bridge and West Bromwich, it does serve to remind one of what might have been. *D. W. K. Jones*

Standing at the terminus of the 87 service, looking in the opposite direction from the previous photograph of 843, with the recently rebuilt Station hotel in the background, is one of the usual UEC-bodied 71 Class trams, in this case car 86. This tram is in total contrast to the last Birmingham tramcar, as it dates back to the Edwardian era. Although sporting the post-1937 BIRMINGHAM CITY TRANSPORT on the rocker panel, it also has a patch there, denoting that by now a more permanent repair was not worthwhile as it will be withdrawn in a few months' time along with the route to Dudley via Smethwick and Oldbury. *W. N. Jackson*

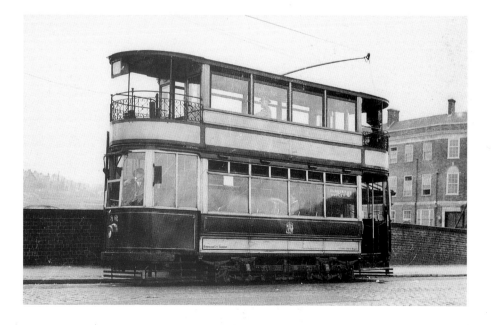

The oldest tramcars in the Birmingham fleet were the 'Aston' bogies. These were originally open-top, 56-seat cars with reversed staircases and open platforms. They were built by the Electric Railway & Tramway Carriage Works Ltd (ER&TCW) in late 1903, entering service from Monday 4 January 1904, at first from Steelhouse Lane to Aston Brook Street, but after 16 June that year the service was run in conjunction with the City of Birmingham Tramways Company as far as Aston Cross.

Car 17 received a UEC-built top-cover in July 1907, and as it was now 16 ft 3 in high it spent most of the remainder of its working life at Miller Street depot working the 6 service through Newtown Row to the terminus at Perry Barr. All the 1-20 Class were transformed in the 1920s when they received EMB bogies, each equipped with Dick, Kerr DK30B 40 hp motors. New half-turn staircases and platform vestibules were fitted in the late 1920s, as were transverse upholstered seats in the lower saloon.

Car 17 was one of only six of the class to survive the war, as most of the Class were destroyed or badly damaged in the air-raid on the night of 9 April 1941. It is seen here unloading in Dale End in the final 1948-style livery, and will then turn right into Martineau Street to reach its city terminus. *C. Carter*

One of the main suburban tramway junctions was at Gravelly Hill; this was the meeting point of three tram services until 4 July 1953 when the Erdington routes were closed and tramcar operation in Birmingham came to an end. It would then have been hard to imagine that today this site would be occupied by a complex of slip-roads and flyovers associated with the elevated M6 Junction 6, perhaps better known as 'Spaghetti Junction'. Car 617 is working on the 78 route and will shortly turn left after the preceding car 670, which on leaving the tram shelters will turn right into Tyburn Road. *T. Marsh*

The extension of the service 1 from Stockland Green along Streetly Road to Short Heath Road was opened on 23 June 1926 and was given the route number 78. The route took the trams into an area of recently constructed council housing, and a terrace of these can be seen behind the Bundy Clock. After the Short Heath route was opened, only three more tramway extensions were to follow. Car 668, a 40 hp Brush-bodied tram of 1924 vintage mounted on EMB maximum-traction bogies, has just arrived at the terminus in the spring of 1953. *I. Davidson*

BIRMINGHAM TRAMS 1933-53

Above On a winter's day early in 1953, car 678 has crossed Chester Road and is approaching the Erdington terminus. It was one of 27 of the 662-701 Class to have survived the Second World War and still be in service during the last year of tramway operation. It spent all its service life based at Miller Street depot and was one of the last trams to be broken up at Kyotts Lake Road in August 1953. *I. Davidson*

Below The 2½-mile-long Tyburn Road from Gravelly Hill to the Pype Hayes terminus at Chester Road was almost all on central reservation track. On its way into the city is car 679, loading up at the Stoneyhurst Road stop with passengers from the factories that lined the south side of Tyburn Road. On the evening of 4 July 1953 car 679 would be the last of the 24 trams to pass through the city centre on its way to Kyotts Lake Road Works for breaking up. *T. Marsh*

Below Freshly repainted in 1949, car 730 waits in Hill Street with the gaunt war-damaged roof of New Street station in the background. The Brush-bodied tram had received some damage when Witton depot received a direct hit from a bomb that resulted in 15 trams being destroyed.

It is seen here about to work on the 37 service to Cannon Hill towards the end of its second spell allocated to Moseley Road depot. It would have the distinction of being the highest numbered Birmingham tram in service when the system finally closed down on 4 July 1953. *C. Carter*

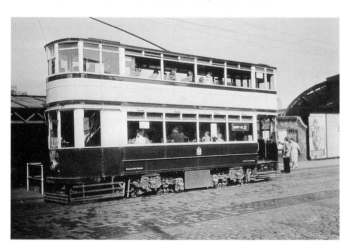

DUDLEY AND WEDNESBURY == VIA WEST BROMWICH AND == GREAT BRIDGE

Hockley, Soho Road and Handsworth

THE ROUTES through Hockley, along Soho Road to Handsworth within the city boundary, including those along Wheeler Street and Grove Lane, had a different historical development from the routes beyond the city boundary to West Bromwich, Wednesbury and Dudley.

The first tramway to be opened within Birmingham was a standard gauge horse-tram service from Monmouth Street (Colmore Row) to Hockley Brook, which was opened to public service on 11 September 1873, only five days after the lease to the Birmingham & District Company was formally agreed on 6 September 1873. This met a line opened outside the town boundary by the same company on Whit Monday 20 May 1872 from Hockley Brook to Hill Top and to Dudley Port. The horse-tram service beyond the New Inns was gradually abandoned over the next two years, but the South Staffordshire & Birmingham District Steam Tramways Co Ltd opened a 3 ft 6 in gauge steam tramway route from Handsworth to Darlaston on 16 July 1883.

On 20 October 1885 the Birmingham Tramways &

Omnibus Co Ltd entered into an agreement with the Patent Cable Tramways Corporation to construct a 3 ft 6 in gauge cable line as far as Hockley Brook. The lease for this was taken over by the Birmingham Central Tramways Co Ltd, which by this time was also operating steam trams on seven routes within the town. This lease included the lines in Great Hampton Row and Wheeler Street, which were opened on 25 October 1886.

The cable route was opened from Colmore Row to Hockley Brook on 24 March 1888 and extended on a second cable to the New Inns on 20 April 1889. The BCT Company was given a 21-year lease to operate both the cable tramway to the New Inns and the accumulator trams along Bristol Road. The cable system was quite successful but did not warrant any further route development.

After the Central company had been taken over by the City of Birmingham Tramways Company on 29 September 1896, it had been anticipated that it would be allowed by Birmingham Corporation to convert all its routes to the newly developed overhead electric system. However, the Corporation would not sanction this and instead applied for Parliamentary powers to operate its own municipal tramway

The Birmingham Central Tramways Company Ltd opened its cable tramway from Colmore Row to Hockley Brook on 24 March 1888 using the Patent Cable Tramways Corporation method of propulsion. The trams were hauled

by one continuous cable on the 1½-mile route. On 20 April 1889 the second section of route to the New Inns at Crocketts Road, Handsworth, was opened. This section was operated by a second cable of about the same length as the original inward part of the route. The brakeman had to be careful when changing cables at Hockley Brook.

Birmingham Central operated 53 cable cars belonging to six classes. This is car 121, which was one of the 119-124 Class built by the Metropolitan Company in 1889 for the Handsworth extension. Metropolitan had pioneered the steel underframed bogie car for steam tram trailers, and the cable cars built at this time were very similar. It is standing outside St Philip's churchyard in the early years of the century, waiting to move off to Hockley Brook. Just visible at the end of Colmore Row are the Corinthian pillars of J. A. Hansom's Town Hall, the construction of which was begun in 1832 and the first concert held there in 1834. *Commercial postcard*

system. Royal Assent was given for this on 11 August 1903 and this further enabled the leases within the city to be taken over on their expiry. Prior to this, in 1901, Handsworth UDC had purchased the cable tram tracks in its area. Steam tram operation ended in the city on 31 December 1906 and the Great Hampton Row tracks were left disused.

On Friday 30 June 1911 the last of the CBT leases in Birmingham expired and the cable tram route as far as Hockley Brook came into the possession of Birmingham Corporation. Handsworth UDC had purchased its section of the cable route on 8 October 1909, then negotiated an operating extension with CBT until the Birmingham section of the lease expired. The cable trams ran for the last time on that Friday evening to be replaced by Corporation electric trams running as far as the Woodman Inn at the Hawthorns boundary with West Bromwich. Strictly speaking the Corporation had no rights to operate outside its boundary, but it overcame this objection by providing the service on behalf of Handsworth Council. The South Staffordshire trams were cut back from the New Inns to the Woodman at the same time. On 9 November 1911 the city was enlarged by the incorporation of Handsworth into Greater Birmingham along with Aston Manor, Erdington, part of Kings Norton and Northfield and Yardley.

Initially Brill open-top cars from the 221 series were used along with newly delivered 301 cars. Until 12 June 1912 these were operated from Miller Street, as Hockley depot was not ready for electric trams because of the conversion from cable traction.

The Corporation lost little time in replacing the long-abandoned steam tram route along Wheeler Street and Lozells Road as far as Villa Cross on 20 November 1912, while Oxhill Road was provided with a service from 20 December of that year. Finally the link from Villa Road to Hockley by way of Hamstead Road was opened on 8 January 1913. A single line in Livery Street was opened on 11 June 1913, which enabled both Corporation trams and the newly introduced Black Country Through Service of the South Staffordshire Tramways (Lessee) Company to run around the perimeter of Snow Hill station from Handsworth as a terminal loop.

When the UEC-built open-balconied bogie cars of the 512-586 Class were delivered at the end of 1913, about 30 went to Hockley. The delivery of Brush-built cars 612-636 in 1920-21 released most of the older trams, enabling the allocation of trams to remain static until the lines outside the boundary were acquired on 1 April 1924. Things were very tight until the 702-731 Class were delivered to Moseley Road depot in 1925, allowing 587-611 to be transferred to Hockley. Similarly, in 1926 new bogie cars at Rosebery Street depot allowed 512-535 to join the others of the Class at Hockley.

All the open-balconied bogie cars in the fleet had their vestibules enclosed in the late 1920s and all Hockley's allocation was re-motored with Dick, Kerr 30/1L 63 hp motors or, in the case of 512-536, GEC WT32R 70 hp motors. This enabled the West Bromwich services to be maintained at a high speed, especially on the long, uninterrupted runs beyond the city boundary.

The route from Colmore Row started outside St Philip's Cathedral and turned into Snow Hill alongside the railway station. On 5 June 1933 the cut-backs caused by the one-way street system meant that all the services entering the city towards Hockley used the Livery Street inbound loop introduced 20 years earlier, and the Colmore Row terminus was abandoned.

Beyond the boundary

On 19 December 1902 the South Staffordshire Tramways (Lessee) Company Ltd opened its electric tram route from the Woodman Inn at the Handsworth boundary to Carter's Green; on 1 April 1903 the company entered into a 21-year lease with West Bromwich to operate trams on the Corporation-owned tracks through the Borough. By 10 April 1903 Wednesbury had been reached. This replaced the steam tram service that had opened on 16 July 1883 from the New Inns, Handsworth, to Darlaston via West Bromwich and Wednesbury, which finally closed on 15 June 1904 after a steam shuttle service had run from the Woodman to the New Inns for nearly 18 months.

South Staffordshire electric trams reached Dudley station from Great Bridge on 30 May 1903 having entered into a new agreement to run electric trams over the Birmingham & Midland Tramways tracks from the junction at Burnt Tree, near Dudley. On 1 October 1904 the South Staffordshire Company was able, after a protracted dispute with Handsworth UDC, to extend its service to the New Inns to meet the CBT cable system.

After the CBT lease expired on 30 June 1911, the new Birmingham Corporation electric service was extended to the new Birmingham boundary at the Woodman Inn, and the South Staffs tramcars were duly cut back from the New Inns to the same point. On 9 October 1912 the South Staffordshire Tramways (Lessee) Co Ltd was able to extend the Darlaston to Handsworth service to Colmore Row and top-covered, 'Aston' type, four-wheel trams were repainted with the legend 'Black Country Through Service' on their rocker-panels.

Later years

Before the West Bromwich Lease was due to expire on 31 March 1924, West Bromwich Corporation approached Birmingham Corporation with the proposal that BCT would 'manage and control' the lines for them. The original intention was that Birmingham Corporation, as well as running the Great Bridge and Dudley route, would run to suitable traffic centres; this meant that the trams would operate beyond the West Bromwich boundary at Holloway Bank, Hill Top, to the White Horse at Wednesbury, where Walsall Corporation and the South Staffordshire Company cars met. It was also suggested that BCT trams would continue to Darlaston and Bilston. The overhead beyond Wednesbury was side-running and in the event, with the indifferent state of the track, Birmingham Corporation only ran as far as Wednesbury, after an unsatisfactory journey with a Hockley bogie car that ran through to Bilston.

In May 1937 West Bromwich decided that it would replace the tram service. The original idea was to do this with trolleybuses from the Birmingham boundary to Dudley and Wednesbury; when Oak Lane depot was

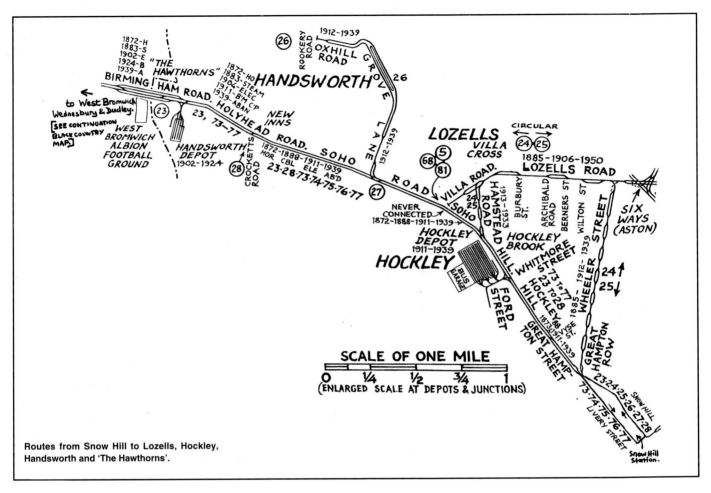

Routes from Snow Hill to Lozells, Hockley, Handsworth and 'The Hawthorns'.

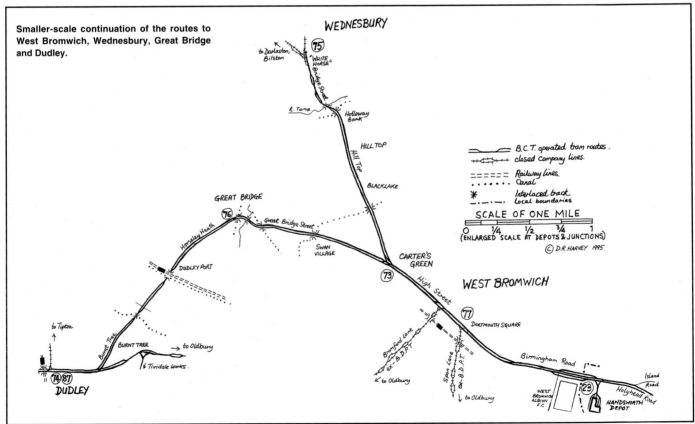

Smaller-scale continuation of the routes to West Bromwich, Wednesbury, Great Bridge and Dudley.

BIRMINGHAM TRAMS 1933-53

rebuilt and enlarged its entrances and roof were built sufficiently high to accommodate trolleybuses, but as West Bromwich wanted to operate a joint service, BCT insisted that diesel-engined buses must be used. Birmingham was originally going to keep open the section of the main line as far as the Woodman as well as the branch services to Wheeler Street and the recently relayed Oxhill Road route. Reluctantly, however, Birmingham decided on complete closure, which would take effect from 2 April 1939.

Route description - Birmingham to the boundary

The trams ran from outside St Philip's Cathedral in Colmore Row, but eventually all services migrated to the loop made by Livery Street, Colmore Row and Snow Hill around the GWR's Snow Hill station. The trams descended Snow Hill, passing on the western side the railway arches beneath the main-line station with their storage spaces deep within the subterranean recesses. Opposite, as far as Great Charles Street, were rows of early-19th-century buildings with a strange assortment of retail outlets including billiard table manufacturers, opticians and rubber goods manufacturers!

Once into Constitution Hill the area changed to one of small tool-making factories. The route climbed towards the Great Hampton Street and Great Hampton Row junction with the inbound cars at Livery Street. The Wheeler Street 24 service turned into a straight, seven-looped run to Lozells Road through an area of Victorian terraces and small shops. At the end of the 1-mile-long stretch of Wheeler Street, the trams turned left into Lozells Road where they joined the 5 route, Birmingham's only inter-suburban tram route. The 24 route went as far as Villa Cross before reversing, but prior to 7 August 1933 this had been the anti-clockwise part of a circular route with the 25 service; this went via Hockley Hill and Hamstead Road before turning into Villa Road and returning to the city by way of Wheeler Street.

Returning to Great Hampton Street, the Hockley-bound trams proceeded through the edge of the Jewellery Quarter and descended into the valley of Hockley Brook. This is where the depot was situated, and in CBT days had been where the cable cars changed cables at the former Birmingham-Handsworth boundary.

Climbing from the shopping centre at Hockley, the trams on the main line passed the turn-off of the 25 route at Hamstead Road at the top of Soho Hill, before reaching Villa Road. This was the terminus of the 5 route, but had never been connected to the Soho Road routes despite an early CBT proposal to link Handsworth with Aston. The Soho Road services then passed over Soho Road station before running past the impressive former town hall of Handsworth UDC and reaching the start of the important shopping centre at Grove Lane.

The 26 route turned right into Grove Lane and passed Handsworth Grammar School on a single-line section before skirting around the western edge of Handsworth Park and running on either side of Birmingham's first dual-carriageway at the end of the 1-mile section of Grove Lane. The trams turned sharp left into Oxhill Road to the terminus at Rookery Road.

The Soho Road services continued through Handsworth's premier shopping area to the turn-back point of the 28 route at the New Inns in Holyhead Road, which had been the terminus of the cable trams until 1911 and the South Staffordshire electric trams from West Bromwich. The trams climbed towards the city boundary and the 23 route terminus at the Woodman public house, which stood near to 'The Hawthorns' ground of West Bromwich Albion FC, and passed the small Handsworth depot, used latterly for up to eight trams which were parked there on match days.

Route description - West Bromwich to Dudley and Wednesbury

At the Woodman was the only stretch of quadruple track on the Birmingham system, laid thus so that on match days trams could be parked on both the kerbside inbound and outbound tracks, thus enabling service trams to proceed normally.

Beyond 'The Hawthorns' was the long straight stretch of track across open country to the residential end of West Bromwich High Street. It was here that the Hockley bogie cars, with their 63 and 70 hp motors, could achieve about 40 mph. Once into West Bromwich High Street, from about Trinity Road the main shopping centre began. The so-called 'Golden Mile' of shops included the important junction at Dartmouth Square; it was here that the Birmingham & Midland single-deck cars ran the Spon Lane shuttle to Smethwick. Spon Lane was the terminus of the 77 service. After continuing past Bromford Lane, along which ran the other B&M single-deck car service, the trams reached Carters Green. At the Farley Clock, nearly opposite the Art Deco-styled Tower Cinema, the 73 route terminated.

The 75 service forked right into Old Meeting Street and climbed through Black Lake before reaching the crest of a steady climb to Hill Top. After passing the early Victorian houses, the trams began the steep descent of Holloway Bank and into the Tame Valley. Wednesbury, one of the heavy industrial centres of the Black Country, was reached at the bottom of Lower High Street at the White Horse public house. Until September 1930 it was possible to see the Company cars on the Darlaston service and Walsall Corporation cars on their service to their home town.

The 74 route left Carters Green via the industrialised landscape of Swan Village to Great Bridge. This district clustered around its Market Place and marked the last short-working from Birmingham, which was numbered 76. The trams took the left fork through Horseley Heath to Dudley Port where the Ryland Aqueduct and the LNWR main line to Wolverhampton crossed the route. In Company days the former could only be negotiated by open-top cars; the overhead was skewed to one side but even so none of the oldest four-wheel trams would pass under the bridge. The route then continued to climb gently to Burnt Tree, but had to negotiate the humped-back bridge over the Birmingham Canal near Sedgley Road.

At Burnt Tree, the 74 route joined the Birmingham & Midland route from Smethwick and Oldbury, running over its tracks to the terminus of both routes on the bridge above Dudley station at the bottom of Castle Hill, Dudley, about 9 miles from Snow Hill.

Snow Hill, Livery Street and Constitution Hill

Left UEC-bodied bogie car 551 arrives at the kerb-side loading terminus at the impressive passenger shelters in Colmore Row. This terminus, a relic from cable car days, was abandoned on 4 June 1933 when Colmore Row became part of Birmingham's famous one-way system; all the Handsworth-bound trams were re-routed via Livery Street to terminate in front of Snow Hill station. Car 551, originally built with open balconies but now totally enclosed, is working the 24 route to Lozells via Wheeler Street.

To the right of this view is St Philip's Cathedral, designed by the Warwickshire architect Thomas Archer in the Baroque style. It was consecrated in 1715 and created a cathedral in 1905. The dedication to St Philip was decided upon because the son of the Colmore family, who were the local landowners, was named Philip, thus making the choice of name as unusual as its elegant and sophisticated design. The splendid row of buildings opposite the cathedral, which survive today, is the Grand Hotel completed in 1875 to the design to J. A. Chatwin. *A. D. Packer collection*

Left The newly reconstructed Snow Hill station stands impressively on the corner of Colmore Row and Livery Street on a bright, sunny afternoon soon after the end of the Great War. Open-balconied car 542 waits at the corner of Livery Street, with its rain-shield being used to shield the driver from the sun. It is working the 23 route to 'The Hawthorns' at the City boundary.

The frontage of Snow Hill was occupied by the Great Western Hotel, completed in 1868 with 120 rooms. Whether the hotel succeeded or not is unknown, but when the GWR become short of office space they approached the lessees who agreed to sell. The Snow Hill station restaurant took over the ground floor by early 1909, while the upper floors became offices. Had it not been for the Second World War, the French chateau-styled building would have been replaced by a six-floor hotel in the 'Kremlin' style of 1930s brutalism.

Snow Hill remained open throughout the time of the Edwardian rebuilding of the station. It required an enormous feat of engineering as the station roof covered a staggering 12,000 square yards. The third Snow Hill station was gradually brought into use and fully opened during January 1912. *Commercial postcard*

Left Car 521 was one of the 75-strong 512 Class that entered service between October 1913 and December 1914, and had a 62-seat UEC open-balconied body. These trams were originally delivered with 28 wooden seats arranged longitudinally in the lower saloon and 34 wooden transverse seats in the upper saloon; the latter had been compared to sitting on a park bench!

By 1939, when this view at the top of Livery Street alongside Snow Hill station was taken, car 521 had been re-motored twice, latterly during 1927 with GEC WT32R 70 hp motors. This tram was one of the Class that received eight-side-windowed top-covers when they had their top vestibules enclosed between July 1929 and November 1930; in this case the work was completed in December 1928. It is working the 28 route to the New Inns. *R. T. Wilson*

BIRMINGHAM TRAMS 1933-53

Right The echo of trams had barely faded when Livery Street was photographed on 11 June 1939. The track is still in situ as are the traction poles, but the trams had officially been withdrawn on 2 April. To the right is Snow Hill station, while opposite are the city centre premises of the Dunlop Rubber Company. The first junction on the left is Cornwall Street and beyond that are the traffic lights that controlled the Great Charles Street junction. In the distance is one of the torque-converted Leyland TD6cs of the 211-295 Class that had recently replaced the trams.

Livery Street is just about half a mile long and took its name from the riding stables that stood near the corner of Cornwall Street on the Colmore Estate. To older Brummies, however, the thoroughfare has another connotation: 'As long as Livery Street' has entered Birmingham folklore as a saying to describe something excessive, such as 'a face as long as. . .'. Well, this is nearly the full length of Livery Street and it isn't particularly long! *R. Carpenter collection*

Middle right This general view of Colmore Row shows an unidentified 512 Class tram, with open balconies, loading up with passengers outside Snow Hill station. The tram will turn left into Snow Hill and descend the hill to the east of the station. The tramcar is fitted with flop-over destination boards and would not have the small route number boxes fitted to the balcony ceiling until after the end of the First World War.

The two capped figures on the extreme right of the view appear to be employees of the tramways department. Behind the rather splendid gas-light lantern on the corner of Livery Street is the entrance archway to Snow Hill station, which led to a tiled booking hall and taxi entrance. In the distance behind the tram can be seen the top of Steelhouse Lane, where the Erdington group of tram routes terminated. The buildings behind the tramcar, on the corner of Bull Street and Steelhouse Lane, were casualties of the redevelopment that took place here in the early 1960s, being replaced by Colmore Circus. *Commercial postcard*

Below right Car 565 was another of the ten 512 Class cars fitted with modified top-saloon windows to the eight-windowed design of the newly delivered 762-811 Class. It stands outside the impressive loading shelters in front of Snow Hill station in March 1939, not long before the change-over to buses. The replacement bus destination signs on top of the shelters are covered over pending the abandonment.

Car 565 had been the subject of a number of motor changes, along with most of the Class, earlier in its career. When built it had been fitted with a Dick, Kerr DK129A double-drive 40 hp motor, which, although suitable for the smaller 301 and 401 Classes, was after a few years beginning to experience an increasing number of failures. Car 565 was fitted in May 1922 with a pair of GEC 249A 37 hp motors of the type then being installed into the 587 Class. These motors, however, quickly became the subject of complaint due to their slow performance and as a result of this, in December 1926, 565 was again re-motored, this time with more powerful Dick, Kerr 30/1L 63 hp motors manufactured by English Electric. It was in this form that the tram ran in service until withdrawal on the last day of tramcar operation in the city on 4 July 1953. Just turning into Snow Hill beneath the General Life building is car 512, working on the 26 route to Oxhill Road. *R. T. Wilson*

Below Tuesday 28 March 1939 sees Brush-bodied car 597 standing at the 74 route loading shelters in Colmore Row in front of Snow Hill station. The tram will shortly be travelling to Dudley on a 9-mile journey via West Bromwich. Note the abandonment poster in the balcony window, which explained the amendments to the services when replaced by Birmingham City Transport Leyland 'Titan' TD6cs and West Bromwich Corporation Daimler COG6s on the following Saturday.

The seemingly impressive permanence of Snow Hill station was also transient, for the electrification of the West Coast Main Line from Euston was to signal the beginning of the end; as early as April 1963 a British Railways spokesman confirmed that it would close on completion of the electrification. Although still busy, over the next four years Snow Hill gradually lost its main-line status, which finally ceased on Saturday 4 March 1967. After that the station had a lingering death, with only local services to Wolverhampton Low Level, Langley Green and Leamington Spa remaining. On 5 May 1969 the once proud station, now with only two platforms, was effectively reduced to an unmanned halt. For many people who remembered the station as a meeting place, or the place from which they went to London on a platform-jammed summer Saturday, it was almost a relief when the nine-year fight to keep it open was finally lost. This occurred on 4 March 1972 when the remaining local services were finally withdrawn.

On 23 October 1969 demolition work began on the former Great Western Hotel, which stands behind tram 597. After Snow Hill was converted to a car park in 1972 the station buildings languished in a state of slow decay until the demolition of the fabric began on 19 May 1977. *L. W. Perkins*

Middle left 1920 Brush-built car 588 stands at the compulsory tram stop alongside Snow Hill station on 28 March 1939, on the short-working to the old cable car terminus at the New Inns, Handsworth. The side goods entrance to platform 12 can be seen to the left of the tram.

The descent of Snow Hill was all the more noticeable because of the ever-higher wall of brickwork that was required to maintain the railway station's level formation across Great Charles Street and the valley of the tiny Fleet Brook.

In common with all the 587-636 Class, car 588 had entered service as an open balcony car with GE 249A 37 hp motors. As more powerful motors were required, the whole Class was fitted with DK301L motors of 63 hp. This enabled the trams to do some very fast running beyond 'The Hawthorns' and in the Great Bridge and Wednesbury areas on the main-line 74 and 75 routes. Although all 50 trams survived the war, 26, including car 588, were withdrawn in October 1950, being made redundant upon the Washwood Heath closure when the EMB air-brake cars of the 762 Class were transferred to Selly Oak. *L. W. Perkins*

Left An unidentified bogie car crosses Constitution Hill and passes into Livery Street on its way into the city on the 24 route from Lozells. It is March 1939 and the Hockley group of routes had only a matter of days before the abandonment on Saturday 1 April. The tram will travel the length of Livery Street, along the western side of Snow Hill station, to the Colmore Row terminus, and is passing in front of the former Great Hampton Picture Palace on the corner of Livery Street and Kenyon Street; this opened in November 1912 and closed in 1932, having probably never been converted to sound films. The building was re-fronted and has been for many years the premises of an electrical engineering company. *J. S. Webb*

BIRMINGHAM TRAMS 1933-53

The 'main line' outbound routes left Constitution Hill and crossed the inbound cars, which effectively went straight on at the Great Hampton Street-Livery Street junction on their way to the Snow Hill station terminus. Car 620 is making this manoeuvre into Livery Street after returning from Wednesbury on the 75 route on Sunday 26 March 1939, and has just rumbled past the W. Canning factory, famous for electro-plating chemicals and machinery. The tram had spent most of its 19 years based on Hockley depot, and it would spend the next nine years at Selly Oak depot working the Bristol Road services, before finally being one of the 66 trams that saw service on the final day of tramcar operation in the city on 4 July 1953. *L. W. Perkins*

Great Hampton Street took the Hockley trams along a thoroughfare lined with metal-spinners, capstan lathe works, brass founders and companies involved in the jewellery trade, for just to the west of this main route is Birmingham's famous Jewellery Quarter. About the time of this photograph, 28 March 1939, in a single square kilometre of the Quarter there were well over 900 workshops.

Brush-built car 615, on the Oxhill Road route, passes Great King Street with Barclays Bank on the corner, while the older UEC trams 558 and 559 are working the 26 and 28 routes, from Oxhill Road and the New Inns respectively. Car 615 would remain in service until the last day of September 1950, but both 558 and 559, despite being six years older, would continue to run on the Erdington routes until July 1953. *L. W. Perkins*

The new bus stop is in place, and the notice has been posted in the end window of Brush-built car 594 that signals the impending abandonment of the 24 route. On 13 March 1939 the tram is about to cross Constitution Hill from Great Hampton Row and make its way along Livery Street to the terminus. Even 2½ years since its last repaint, the gold-lined-out livery, which gave the pre-war Birmingham tramcar its dignified appearance, still looks very tidy.

Behind the horse and cart and the small Bedford lorry is the Minerva public house; this was an Atkinson house, whose advertisement can be seen on the end wall of the premises. In this commercial inner city area, the only private vehicle appears to be the stationary Standard Flying Ten, which is parked beside the wire factory owned by Parsonages. *H. B. Priestley*

Lozells

Above After the trams had passed along Wheeler Street, they then turned left into Lozells Road opposite St Paul's church to the busy shopping centre with its many small shops; suburban shopping centres such as these were a hive of activity. Larger retail outlets such as Taylors the Chemist were part of a city-wide chain of shops, but it was the smaller privately owned shops like tobacconists, corn-dealers, drapers and ladies' outfitters that gave Lozells and other out-of-town shopping centres their separate identities.

Trams 514 and 614 stand in Lozells Road at the junction of Lozells Street late in 1938. Despite their destination blinds, both are working the 24 route, as the 25 blind was being displayed for the benefit of the photographer, five years after that service had closed.

Car 614 is working towards Villa Cross via Wheeler Street and is about half a mile away from the terminus. It is being followed by an almost new Standard Flying Fourteen motor car.

Behind tram 514 is an open-balconied 301 Class tramcar, which is working the 5 route from Villa Road to Gravelly Hill. The traffic congestion is not being helped by the 1938 Morris Eight two-door saloon parked outside Nos 123 and 125 Lozells Road. *W. A. Camwell*

Left Brush-built car 600 stands at the terminus of the 24 route in Lozells Road next to the Villa Cross public house. Originally the 24 route ran on an anti-clockwise circular from Constitution Hill via Great Hampton Row, Wheeler Street, Lozells Road, Villa Road, Hamstead Road and back to the city via Hockley Hill. The 25 route ran in the reverse direction, but after the latter service was abandoned on 7 August 1933, the tracks beyond Villa Cross were only used in service by the 5 route, which went up Villa Road to the junction with Soho Road, although unlike in horse-tram days it was never linked to that main-line route.

To the right of the tram is the large Gothic-styled, late-19th-century church standing on the corner of George Street, which dwarfs the surrounding houses and shops. On the corner of George Street is a red fire alarm just outside the corn merchants. Parked next to the traction pole is a butcher's boy's delivery bicycle belonging to Tisdales shop. *R. T. Wilson*

Hockley

Right The main route through to Handsworth was at one time operated by the Birmingham Central Tramways Company, which opened its cable tramcar route on 24 March 1888 as far as Hockley, where the first part of the cable ended. On 20 April 1889 the outer half of the route was opened to the New Inns. The cars had to change cables at Hockley Brook and here cable car 79, one of the original 1888 trams built by Falcon (later Brush) of Loughborough stands at the junction with Farm Street, opposite Whitmore Street, where the depot was situated. The tram driver is apparently moving the cable-gripper levers.

This view, taken about 1895, is somewhat a mystery. The lower saloon has drawn curtains and the tram is displaying two signs, FULL and the letter 'R'. Could this mean 'Reserved'? Strangely, the only passenger appears to be the elderly gentleman with the top-hat on the upper saloon.

The mid-19th-century buildings on the northeast side of Hockley Brook still have the vestiges of Regency-styled housing above their pediments. *Newman College*

Right Some 45 years later, on Friday 31 March 1939, these buildings still remained, but they were all swept away when Hockley flyover was built in the 1970s. Three trams, led by cars 548 and 534, descend Soho Hill to meet the junction with Farm Street on their way towards the city. Car 548 is working the 26 service from Oxhill Road, while car 534 is on the 28 service from the New Inns at Handsworth.

To the left are the tracks leading into Whitmore Street and to Hockley depot. It was here, in cable tram days, that the depot had to employ steam locomotives to push the cable cars out on to the main line where they could be attached to the cable.

In the distance can be seen the tram stop shelter in the middle of the junction with Claremont Road. The shelter was a recent addition, having been built in 1935. In the foreground the Smethwick-registered Standard Flying Ten waits to lead an Austin Ruby Seven across the junction when the point-duty policeman gives his signal. By the end of this weekend this apparently normal 'tramscape' will be no more. *H. B. Priestley*

Right On every system in Britain, works cars tended to lead somewhat secretive lives; they worked at night or were called out on duties to repair track or overhead wires, or to delivery sand, ballast or other essential materials. They swung out of side roads and disappeared into obscure recesses of the tramway network that passenger cars rarely saw.

This car was built in 1907 by Milnes, Voss on Brill 21E trucks as a stores van. In August 1924 it was converted to a tower-wagon and was numbered 01. It was used at Hockley depot to assist in dismantling the overhead wiring when the depot was being converted to operate buses, and as a result had the dubious distinction of being the last tram to leave the depot on 18 May 1939. It is seen turning into the depot from Whitmore Street in March 1939. *J. S. Webb*

Above Standing at the entrance to Hockley depot in March 1939 are tramcars 183, 623, 602 and 533. Car 183 was one of the last of the ex-Radial open-balconied four-wheelers to remain in active service at the depot. It had only recently arrived at the depot by February 1939, having been in service at Coventry Road depot on the Stechford routes. It would soon go to Rosebery Street depot until its withdrawal from service in September 1939.

Some of the engineering staff at Hockley are posing between the four tramcars on tracks 5 to 8 in valedictory stance before the closure of the depot. The oldest of the bogie cars, the UEC-bodied car 533 mounted upon Mountain & Gibson Burnley bogies and fitted by now with powerful GEC WT32R 70 hp motors, was transferred to Moseley Road depot until

December 1941. Brush-built cars 602 and 623, the latter destined to become Birmingham's penultimate tramcar in July 1953, went to Selly Oak depot in April 1939 to work on the Bristol Road services. *W. A. Camwell*

Below Roads 1 to 4 in Hockley depot were occupied by a wide range of tramcars in this 1925 view. On the right, one of the large 62-seater Brush-built bogie cars, 618, still to have its balcony enclosed, exemplifies the type of tram that was used for main-line and all-day duties. This 63 hp tram would survive until October 1950.

The next two roads are headed by ex-CBT trams. Car 490, a Brush-built 'Aston' type originally with Lycett & Conaty 8 ft 6 in radial trucks, was formerly CBT 227. This tram was top-covered and vestibuled in 1924 and ran until May 1938. Car 472 was ex-CBT 242 and had been built at CBT's Kyotts Lake Road Works in 1904. Originally, like all the ex-CBT tramcars, an open-top tram, it was taken over in January 1912 wearing the Company's Corinthian green and pale yellow livery, unlike 490, which retained the Munich lake and primrose livery that had been superseded in 1909. Car 472 was also rebuilt in 1924 and lasted in service until June 1938.

The final tram is car 56, one of the Brill Class that were built in 1906. It had been fitted with the Maley track brake at the end of that decade, after a fatal accident in October 1907 on Warstone Lane hill when car 22 overturned. The UEC bodies were top-covered, but car 56 had yet to be vestibuled, which further helps to date the view. Just visible on the left is one of the stores vans, possibly 6, built by Milnes, **Voss**. *D. R. Harvey collection*

Picking up passengers at the Claremont Road shelters on its outward journey on the 26 route to Oxhill Road is UEC-built car 544. It is carrying the blue '*Evening Despatch*' advertisement on the balcony dash-panel; this paper was published from 1902 before finally closing in 1963 after being taken over by the *Birmingham Post and Mail*. The tram would also be soon replaced, in this case by buses. Birmingham Corporation ordered 85 Leyland TD6cs to replace about 110 trams allocated to Hockley depot. West Bromwich Corporation initially ordered 31 Daimler COG6s as part of its share in the operation of the Handsworth and West Bromwich services. Hockley garage also ran the Dudley Road routes with the 1270-1319 Class of Leyland 'Titan' TD6cs after October 1939, giving it a total allocation of some 150 buses, which meant that there was a potential capacity problem at the garage after the trams had been withdrawn. *R. T. Wilson*

The climb up Soho Hill from Hockley was quite steep, and here car 556, one of the Mountain & Gibson UEC-bodied trams delivered in 1914, ascends the gradient on its way to Oxhill Road. Having left Hockley Brook, it has just passed the large silversmith Atlas Works of Adie Brothers and will travel straight on past Hamstead Road junction and continue into Soho Road.

Most of the buildings in this view, which was taken from the top-deck of a city-bound tram, have been demolished and the scene is now dominated by Hockley flyover, built to relieve pressure on the junction with the Inner Circle bus route and what was later to become part of the Middle Ring Road scheme. *H. B. Priestley*

The Bull-nosed Morris Cowley dates this view around the middle of the 1920s. The tree-lined Hamstead Road was used by the 24 and 25 routes until the summer of 1933, then remained in use for depot journeys until 1939. This short section of the circular service became only the fourth to close, after Nechells, Bolton Road and Hagley Road. The single-line track had above it, as usual, two wires to cater for trams operating in both directions. In the distance is an open-balconied 512 Class bogie car; it is going away from the road junction in the foreground and is therefore working on the 25 route. It has just passed the graceful tower of Hamstead Road Baptist Church, built in 1883 in Hamstead stone with a light stone dressing that enriched the heavy Gothic decorated windows of the nave. Most of the buildings in this scene remain today, although traffic conditions are somewhat different and the trees have mostly disappeared. *Commercial postcard*

Below For a short time after the conversion from CBT's cable trams to Birmingham Corporation's trams on 1 July 1911, the electric cars ran on lightweight cable track that had been bonded to ensure an earth return. The open-topped 221 Class operated this route in the main until the replacement electric tram track could be laid. By the time this photograph was taken, the cable track and its centre slot had been removed and 301 Class cars were the mainstay of the service. The Corporation trams went as far as the Handsworth/West Bromwich boundary at 'The Hawthorns', where they met the open-topped bogie cars of the South Staffordshire Company. These were in such poor condition by the time that they were withdrawn that they were given the nickname of the 'Darley Nags'.

After the cable depot was cleared it took until 12 June 1912 to convert Hockley for electric cars, and until that time the route was operated by trams from Miller Street and Handsworth depots. Some 301 Class cars were then allocated to the re-opened Hockley depot. By the end of 1913 bogie cars of the 512 Class, then brand new, were operating on the Handsworth services and the smaller 301 Class cars that had gone to Hockley depot 18 months earlier moved away.

Almost new UEC top-covered car 370 runs over new track in Soho Road early in 1913. The tram is outside Handsworth Council House having reached its destination as the flop-over board on the canopy reads STAFFORD ROAD TO COLMORE ROW. This short-working was later given the route number 27.

The Frighted Horse public house is on the corner of Stafford Road beyond the Council House where the little boy holding his dad's hand is walking. It is selling Cheshire's Windmill Ales but was taken over by M&B in 1914. *Commercial postcard*

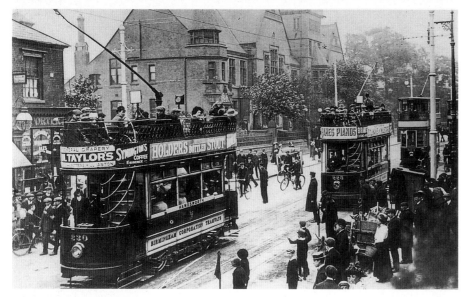

Middle left On Saturday 1 July 1911 electric trams replaced the CBT cable cars through Handsworth UDC from Birmingham. Outside Handsworth Council House, seen behind the trams, a crowd of people stand watching the passage of the new cars. Car 230 has returned from the Woodman Inn at the Handsworth boundary.

Fiercely independent of Birmingham's influence, Handsworth had been in Staffordshire, and regarded itself as part of the Black Country. The foundation stone of the Council House was laid on 30 October 1877, but this further example of civic pride was to lead a truncated life in its original role as the UDC's headquarters when the district was incorporated into Birmingham. It survives today as Handsworth library.

Car 230 carries an advertisement for Holders Stout, which was brewed in Nova Scotia Street; Ashted and Cheshires Brewery, which licensed the Frighted Horse pub immediately behind the tram, were both taken over by M&B.

Car 225 is passing a cross-over that had been laid into the old cable track to enable cars to turn back at Stafford road; the cable conduit can be seen between the lines. Just visible is top-covered car 324, which was only about two months old. *D. R. Harvey collection*

Below left Car 514 leaves the Soho Road junction with Grove Lane after turning towards the city when working the 216 from Oxhill Road. The junction, although important, was not then controlled by traffic lights as the quantity of cross traffic in this early 1930s scene did not warrant such measures. In the background the tower of Handsworth Council House dominates the skyline, while the row of buildings along Soho Road has not yet been totally converted to retail use. The double-fronted early Victorian house, just behind the last two children crossing the main road, is still protected by a small brick wall surmounted by iron railings; it was later converted into a Westminster Bank. The change of use of premises along main roads varied enormously according to the pressures that were being made on an area. *Commercial postcard*

Oxhill Road branch

Above It is 27 September 1938, the day that the liner *Queen Elizabeth* was launched at John Brown's Clydebank yard. Car 601, by now fitted with Dick, Kerr DK30/1L 63 hp motors coupled to the original Brush-built Burnley maximum traction bogies, turns from Grove Lane into Soho Road. On the corner of Grove Lane is Dudleys furniture store, whose armchair sign graced the corner of the shop for many years. The Soho Road shopping centre can be seen in the distance.

On this quiet sunny Tuesday afternoon, another tram is travelling on the 28 route short-working to the New Inns. It is being masked by a 30 cwt van, and in the foreground, just crossing the junction, is a 1937 Ford Y-type Tudor saloon; its VP registration was the only Birmingham-allocated combination that did not include an 'O' in it, and had been added to the 16 'O'-combination Birmingham marks in the 1920s. After 1937 and for many years, VP was usually used for commercial vehicles. *W. A. Camwell*

Right Looking into Grove Lane from Soho Road, two apparently identical tramcars are working on the Oxhill Road route. Car 519 has the more powerful GEC WT32R 70 hp motors while car 553, partly obscured by the two children, is fitted with DK30/1L 63 hp motors. It is Friday 31 March 1939 and on the following day all the Handsworth routes will be abandoned.

This photograph was nearly a failure. The two young pedestrians have nearly hidden the number of one of the tramcars, and while the cyclist to the right has just cleared the scene, the tram entering the photograph on the left will in about one second completely obscure both trams! *H. B. Priestley*

GROVE LANE, HANDSWORTH. (41) G.209.

Once into Grove Lane the route became single-track between Union Row and Dawson Road. Car 619 is passing Handsworth Grammar School for Boys some time in the mid-1930s; this had opened in August 1862 as the Bridge Trust School and became the Grammar School in 1890. The 1934 Ford Y type car is registered in Dundee; in pre-motorway days that was a considerable drive. *Commercial postcard*

The open-balconied 512 Class tramcar has just passed Holly Road in Grove Lane travelling towards the city. The rider of the motor cycle combination is apparently talking to the occupant of his side-car, rather than paying attention to avoid getting the spindly tyres of his steed caught up in the tram tracks! 'Mack Sennett comedy' incidents like that were all too regular an occurrence and the end result could be extremely unpleasant.

A Model T Ford van is unloading outside Harold Honeychurch's bakery shop. In later years the premises became a doctor's surgery and more recently a raincoat manufacturers. The late-19th-century terraced houses represented the last phase of Victorian growth in the Birmingham area. Similar houses with bay windows and walled front gardens could be found in areas such as Moseley, Sparkhill and Small Heath. *Commercial postcard*

Just prior to the route's abandonment, car 548 of 1914 vintage, mounted upon Mountain & Gibson Burnley bogies, prepares to drop down the hill from the compulsory stop at Holly Lane in Grove Lane into the small valley of Farcroft Brook. Behind it the battery-electric bread van crawls up the hill beneath the high brick wall of 63-acre Handsworth Park, opened in 1889 and almost inevitably originally known as Victoria Park. It had been part of the Grove Estate, which had at its northern end the parish church of St Mary's in which are buried three of the founding fathers of the Industrial Revolution, Matthew Boulton, James Watt and William Murdoch. Divided by the Soho and Perry Barr railway line, for many years the park was used for large annual shows, searchlight tattoos and Boy Scout Jamborees, but is now better known as the home of the Handsworth Festival. The trams only skirted the park for about 300 yards as Grove Lane swung away to the north-west and climbed up out of the valley towards Oxhill Road. *R. T. Wilson*

BIRMINGHAM TRAMS 1933-53

When part of Grove Lane was widened for the laying of the tramlines, it was made a dual-carriageway. The existing trees remained on what became the central reservation, with the tramlines running on either side, a unique arrangement in Birmingham. Standing on the corner of Grove Lane and Oxhill Road is the Grove public house, opened in 1891. The scene has changed remarkably little in the intervening years, although the houses in College Road beyond the Methodist church have mostly been converted to small shops.

Still with its open balconies but fitted with balcony route number boxes, the unidentified 512 Class tram has just turned from Grove Lane and is about to travel the last quarter of a mile to the terminus. *Commercial postcard*

The Oxhill Road service was opened on 20 November 1912 and altered little before abandonment on 1 April 1939. The terminus, at the junction of Stockwell Road (to the left) and Rookery Road (to the right), was a single-line stub, in which waits Brush-built car 590. It has had its trolley-pole turned prior to returning to the city. In the background another tram waits on the double-track to gain access to the stub.

The 25-mile Outer Circle bus route turned from Rookery Road along the Oxhill Road section of the Ring Road, which was labelled as such on the lamp posts around the route; the diamond shaped 'Ring Road' sign may be seen on the lamp-post in this view. The houses in Oxhill Road were built at the end of the 19th century on what had been farmland owned by Oxhill Farm. Part of the open landscape escaped housing development by becoming parts of Handsworth Cemetery and Handsworth golf course.

The Standard Flying Twelve motor car is parked outside the row of shops at the terminus. The half-timbered shop with the corner lantern looks as though it has pretensions to be a public house. Outside Smiths tobacconist shop is an early vending machine, possibly for cigarettes, as the sign above it has the well-known 'Players Please' slogan. *Commercial postcard*

Looking away from the city in March 1939, the rest of Oxhill Road can be seen continuing beyond the right of tramcar 620 towards the Uplands Hotel public house and Sandwell Road. The tram is in the same position as in the last picture. Car 620 would eventually work until the last day of the system, having run about 950,000 miles in service. It was broken up in July 1953 at Witton depot.

In 1939 the 3½-mile tram journey from Colmore Row was 2½d, with the first tram of the day starting at 5.31 am. The 26 route would be replaced by the 70 bus service, which was extended to the Uplands Hotel, some half a mile away. *J. S. Webb*

Handsworth

Left The main line along Soho Road beyond Grove Lane climbed through the busy shopping centre. This view, looking from the city, shows Rookery Road to the right, just beneath the sign for Yates boot and shoe shop, and Queens Head Road to the left.

Car 629 is coming downhill on the 28 route from the New Inns terminus about 600 yards away. It has just passed the Regal Cinema on the left and is at the compulsory stop opposite the M&B-owned Queens Head public house. The tram will run down through Soho Road's shopping centre, which was the main one for Handsworth.

Opposite the tram, parked facing out of the city, is a horse-drawn milk float whose milkman appears to be stranded on the other side of the road. Withers newsagents, just behind the FROM CITY tram stop on the left, seems to have a stainless steel vending machine next to the newspaper hoardings. The motor car in the foreground, parked on the wrong side of the road, is a 1934 OC-registered Standard Ten. *Commercial postcard*

Left On Guy Fawkes night 1938, at 7.08 pm at the height of the evening rush hour, there was a power failure on Soho Road. Outside the Regal Cinema on the corner of Booth Street the trams stood like beached whales, all the way through Handsworth as far as the eye could see. It took about an hour to clear the problem, by which time the passengers had abandoned ship and walked home, somewhat disgruntled at their misfortune.

Here tram 602, built in 1920 by the Brush Company of Loughborough, passes the Regal Cinema in about 1934, the site of which is today a Kwik Save supermarket. The cinema was opened on Sunday 13 October 1928 with a live stage show. On the following day it showed its first film, *Paris Bound*. The cinema was designed by Harold Seymour Scott, who was responsible for seven other Birmingham picture houses, including The Oak at Selly Oak and the Pavilion at Wylde Green. However, the Regal was the biggest; with 2,150 seats it was the largest suburban cinema in the city and was also the first equipped from new for the 'Talkies'. As the ABC Handsworth, it finally closed on 16 November 1968. *Commercial postcard*

Left The original CBT cable tram terminus was at the New Inns, Handsworth, visible here with its prominent clock. After the opening of the Corporation electric service on 1 July 1911, the New Inns became a short-working of the 23 route, which continued to the West Bromwich boundary at the Woodman public house, near 'The Hawthorns' football ground.

In the distance is a South Staffordshire Tramways (Lessee) Company tramcar identifiable by its triangular screen beneath the vestibule window. It is working the 'Black Country Through Service' from Darlaston to Colmore Row, dating this view to before April 1924 when BCT took over the West Bromwich routes.

Corporation car 64, one of the Brill 21E-trucked cars of 1905, stands outside the New Inns on the 28 route. It was rebuilt with a top-cover and Maley track brakes before the First World War. *Commercial postcard*

Right Standing at the New Inns in late March 1939 is UEC car 556. On the tram standard are a number of signposts, the top one reading 'Smethwick 1½ (miles)'.

The hazard of boarding a tram in the middle of the road was negligible, though with parked cars lining the roads today, passengers face similar problems, though for different reasons!

The New Inns public house was built for Mitchell & Butlers in 1901, though its huge Assembly Room was not finished until 1904. The interior was decorated with Art Nouveau ceramic tiles and was regarded as being one of the gems of interior public house design in the Birmingham area. There had been a hostelry on this site for 600 years, but after remaining derelict for many years it was refurbished and converted to flats at the end of November 1995. *R. T. Wilson*

Middle right The tramcar is standing at the same spot as car 556 in the previous picture, but the photograph is taken looking away from the city. Car 597, later to become the last passenger tramcar to be broken up, is working the 74 route from Dudley on Friday 31 March 1939.

Behind the tram is the Albion Cinema, which had been opened in December 1915. It had a seating capacity of 800, but had the unique feature of being able to accommodate another 300 people waiting to see the next picture! It closed in 1961. *H. B. Priestley*

Below left The small South Staffordshire Tramways Albion depot on the Handsworth boundary in Holyhead Road was built by the South Staffordshire Company and opened on 20 December 1902. After 1924 it was used only as parking space for up to eight trams when West Bromwich Albion were playing at home.

The stores van 6 would be parked there on match days to supply conductors with new stocks of tickets. This van had been the last of six built in January 1907; mounted on Mountain & Gibson 21E trucks, it had been fitted with a jib and hoist for lifting heavy goods. These had been removed in 1913 and after that it spent most of its life at Hockley. When that depot closed, van 6 went to the works for store and was broken up in 1945. In March 1939 some of the platform staff pose in front of cars 553 and 598. Albion depot closed on 2 April 1939 and the premises were converted to industrial use. *D. R. Harvey collection*

Below right Albion depot has been rebuilt at the Black Country Museum in Dudley, after 50 years being used as a factory, to house the small opera-

tional fleet of mainly Tividale-built single-deck tramcars owned by the Museum. Some of the bricks for the reconstructed tram depot, made at the same brickworks, came from a demolished hospital site in Dudley. However it retains the spirit of the tram depot, austere in its blue bricks and as tall and gaunt as the trams that were finally housed in it, and will make a splendid addition to the Museum, which captures the feel of the Black Country in the early years of this century. *D. R. Harvey*

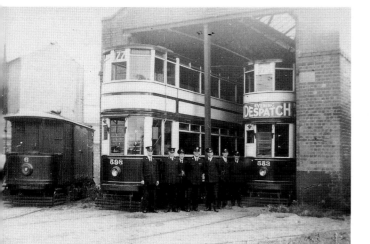

Across the boundary to West Bromwich

Top The Woodman public house, partly visible behind the line of trams, marked the boundary between Handsworth and West Bromwich. It was here, from 20 December 1902, that the South Staffordshire Tramway (Lessee) Company started electric trams to Dudley and Darlaston. At the boundary was 'The Hawthorns' football ground, home of West Bromwich Albion; their ground is situated between Halfords Lane and the Birmingham boundary. The club had been formed by workers from the Salters Spring factory in 1879. Like Aston Villa, West Bromwich Albion was a founder member of the Football League, set up in 1888. The club moved into 'The Hawthorns' on 3 September 1900.

In 1924 the tracks in Birmingham Road were quadrupled so that football specials could be parked alongside the kerb while the normal service cars used the two centre tracks. It was the only place on the Birmingham system where four street tracks were laid side by side.

On Saturday 1 April 1939 a line-up of trams led by car 542, followed by 514, 517 and 636, before the gap to 616, stands awaiting the crowds from a reserve match at 'The Hawthorns'. *L. W. Perkins*

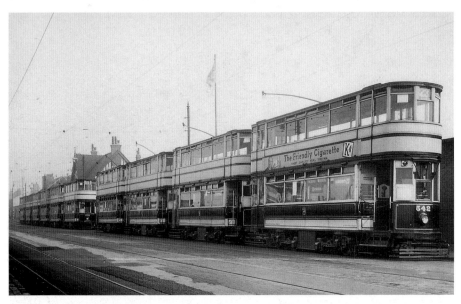

Middle left Both sides of the main Birmingham Road looking towards Handsworth are occupied by Corporation tramcars waiting on the kerb-side tracks for the crowds to leave the football ground. It is Saturday 25 March 1939 and 'The Baggies', who had been relegated to the Second Division the season before, were playing Fulham in front of a crowd of 19,541 fans; they won 3-0. This was the last first team home match at 'The Hawthorns' served by tramcars.

Just visible is a tram on normal service running along the central track towards West Bromwich. It has just left the Woodman after the driver has 'pegged' at the Bundy Clock. Passengers on through journeys were not able to through-book their tickets if they were crossing the boundary but had to pay again from 'The Hawthorns'; this practice continued until 27 August 1967. The word 'Boundary' seemed only to be used on the CBT system to describe 'The Hawthorns'.

If the memory of Saturdays in Birmingham Road was of the unique parking arrangements for the trams, then for the rest of the week it was the wonderful aroma of freshly baked bread that emanated from Bradford's bakery to the left of the parked cars. *J. S. Webb*

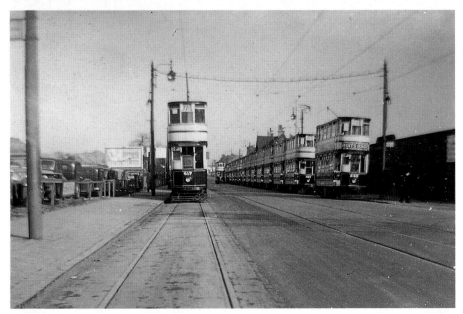

Below left After the publication of the Taylor Report on football ground safety, the recommendation to have all-seat stadia was acted upon by the larger clubs. Although West Bromwich Albion was not in the Premiership League, it obviously had aspirations to be there and as a result decided to invest in the rebuilding of its ground to meet the new requirements.

Leyland 'Fleetline' 6710 (SDA 710S), built in 1978 with a Metro-Cammell body for West Midlands PTE, passes the almost complete Birmingham Road stand at the end of July 1994. A Volvo articulated lorry passes the end of Halfords Lane while at the far end of the new stand can be glimpsed the mock-Tudor gables of the Woodman public house. The new cantilevered stand is far removed from the old pre-war banking behind the goals, but is now deemed necessary to supply the discerning soccer fan with something more than aching feet and a cup of Bovril and a meat pie at half-time. *D. R. Harvey*

BIRMINGHAM TRAMS 1933-53

Passing the garage, which is selling second-hand Austin 7 hp cars for as little as £24, are trams 523, a UEC-built tram of 1914, and car 636, the last of the 50 Brush-built 587 Class of 1920. Both trams had been built with open balconies but had been enclosed in the late 1920s. The newer tramcar is returning to Hockley depot while 523 is working on the 23 route to City. This 1939 view was taken at the Woodman public house looking away from the city. *W. A. Camwell*

Seen from the top-deck of another tram on 31 March 1939, car 565 speeds across the long flat, straight section of the tram route towards West Bromwich when working the Wednesbury route. This was a section of route on which the trams could be notched-up and really exhibit the performance available to the higher-horse-power cars. This 63 hp tram was probably more than a match for the small Thornycroft lorry it is overtaking. The area to the right at this time was largely undeveloped, while to the left was the home of Dartmouth Cricket Club, for many years a major force in Birmingham League cricket. *H. B. Priestley*

Once across the Sandwell Valley, Birmingham Road became High Street just before Roebuck Lane. Here, large gabled villas and terraces had been built in the last decade of the 19th century as the town expanded eastwards towards Birmingham. This expansion was indirectly encouraged by the opening on 16 July 1883 of the Handsworth (New Inns), West Bromwich, Wednesbury and Darlaston steam tram service of the South Staffordshire & Birmingham District Steam Tramways Co Ltd.

The combination of Beyer, Peacock steam tram loco number 3, built in 1883, and one of the large Starbuck 60-seat trailers must have been an impressive sight as it hissed along its route. The tram is passing Bagnall Street in about 1900. The turreted house on the extreme left of the photograph still stands, although the steam trams on this section of the route were withdrawn on 19 December 1902 and replaced by South Staffordshire electric cars. *D. R. Harvey collection*

With Marks & Spencers and Burtons in the background, totally enclosed bogie car 545 passes Dartmouth Square in West Bromwich High Street on 31 March 1939, working on the 74 route from Dudley to Birmingham. Dartmouth Square, which was the heart of West Bromwich, was named after the Earls of Dartmouth, the Legge family, who moved to Sandwell Hall in 1701. Where the tram stands is the present-day site of the Farley Centre, while the High Street is now pedestrianised between Dartmouth Square and St Michael's Street. The only building to survive is Burtons, in its usual 'house style' of 1930s Art Deco. On the same side of the High Street, behind the tram, is the site of the grocery and tea-dealing establishment opened by Joseph Parker in 1834. This was a predecessor of the country's first George Mason grocery chain shop.

Car 545 went to Selly Oak depot by June 1939, but was stored after collision damage from December 1940 until May 1946! Even after return to service, it didn't last long, being finally taken out of service in July 1950. *H. B. Priestley*

Viewed from Paradise Street with bunting for a pageant celebration, or perhaps even Coronation decorations, as it appears to be about 1937, a Dennis 'Lance' II bus, one of four delivered to West Bromwich Corporation in 1934 and fitted with modern-looking metal-framed MCCW bodies, disappears into High Street. Alongside it is the small traffic island that carried the splendid Town Clock and had beneath it more prosaic subterranean lavatories. The clock was cast by Salters in 1912 and stands in very much the same position today.

On the way in from Handsworth is a BCT bogie car working on the 74 route to Dudley. Behind it is the splendid 'mish-mash' of building styles that always seemed to be one of the more endearing qualities of the High Street.

To the right of the tram, on the corner of Spon Lane, is the Dartmouth Hotel, which was the terminus for the Spon Lane tram service. Until 17 November 1929 the Birmingham District Company ran single-deck, Tividale-built, four-wheel trams along Spon Lane to West Smethwick, with car 2 operating the last journey. *P. Spencer*

HIGH STREET, WEST BROMWICH.

In this 1929 view, and identifiable by its balcony advertisement for 'Best Value for Fireplaces', car 548, on its way from Wednesbury to Birmingham and passing through the main shopping centre of West Bromwich. The tram has just passed St Michael's Street, which is still wired up for the Birmingham & District single-deck tram route to Oldbury via Bromford Lane, which closed on 17 November 1929.

The policeman, who is wearing white gloves, is on point-duty just to the front of the tramcar; he has been passed by a rather splendid mid-1920s Standard car. *Commercial postcard*

BIRMINGHAM TRAMS 1933-53

Right Birmingham & Midland single-deck combination car 62 stands in Bromford Lane when working the Oldbury shuttle service in about 1929. This tram, built at Kyotts Lake Road Works in 1904, had returned to the B&M in 1926 after having been transferred to the Dudley-Stourbridge section in 1911. It therefore had only about 2½ years on the 'Lanes' services in West Bromwich before the routes were abandoned. The tram is leaving St Michael's Street, West Bromwich, having just begun its journey to Oldbury. *A. Jensen collection*

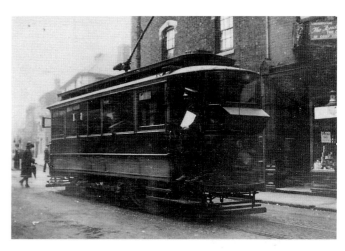

Middle right On a rainy Saturday in 1938, car 533 travels along West Bromwich High Street towards Birmingham, working on the 73 route from Carters Green. The driver is using the tram's rain-shield; Birmingham tramcars were not fitted with the luxury of windscreen wipers and this usage of the shield by the drivers was the way in which vision was improved in rainy conditions. The tram has just passed the junction with New Street. In the background the tall building belongs to Kenrick & Jefferson (K&J), one of the largest printing companies in Britain, making stationery, calendars and greetings cards.

In 1937 the West Bromwich undertaking started to purchase oil-engined buses from a number of different manufacturers for evaluation purposes. The double-deck bus in this view is one of these, numbered 64 (EA 9001), a Daimler COG6 with a 56-seat Metro-Cammell body. It proved to be the precursor of some 35 similar buses purchased in 1939 and 1940 for tram replacement purposes, and could always be recognised as it was the only COG6 in the fleet to have the area beneath the front number plate painted blue and not cream. It is working a Football Special from Stone Cross via Tantany to 'The Hawthorns', and is being passed by a small Dennis 'Ace' with a locally built 20-seat W. D. Smith body. *D. R. Harvey collection*

Below Travelling along West Bromwich High Street is Brush-built car 520. This 70 hp car would later see service on the wide-open spaces of the Bristol Road central reservation, but is seen here having just reversed at the St Michael's Street terrace of shops dating from the mid-19th century, which include the Warwickshire household furnishing shop. They are indulging in a somewhat transatlantic sales campaign by which their prices are being 'Slaughtered'. Behind the tram is the Sandwell public house with its wonderfully self-indulgent Victorian frontage. *W. A. Camwell*

Carters Green

Right At Carters Green the two tram routes diverged, with the 74 route forking slightly to the left through to Great Bridge and Dudley, while the 75 route forked to the right at the clock tower and went via Hill Top to Wednesbury.

Service number 73 was allocated to the short-working that terminated at Carters Green. Car 596, trolley-pole turned for the return run to Birmingham, is standing outside the Tower Cinema, opened on 9 December 1935. Its first film was Robert Donat and Madeleine Carroll in Alfred Hitchcock's classic version of *The Thirty-nine Steps*. Although of French-Irish parents, Madeleine Carroll was born in West Bromwich in 1906 and it was very appropriate that this film should have been shown as the cinema's first feature.

It is 9 August 1938 and the cinema has as its main film *The Buccaneer* starring Fredric March and Akim Tamiroff. The cinema, with its splendid Art Deco front, closed in 1968 and after a period as a bingo hall was demolished in the 1980s. Car 596 survived until December 1952 when it was withdrawn with flatted wheels and split pinions. *W. A. Camwell*

Below The end is in sight for the trams, with abandonment notices on their windows and a replacement bus 'hovering' in the background. On 31 March 1939 car 522 approaches the junction at the Farley Clock at Carters Green and will take the tracks to its left as it goes towards Dudley. Behind it is Leyland 'Titan' TD6c bus 271 (EOC 271), one of the fleet that was purchased to replace the tram services to West Bromwich. The buses were

built with torque-converted transmission that effectively meant that they were automatics. This was an advantage for tram drivers learning to drive buses, but there were disadvantages; the added weight of the transmission meant that their MCCW bodies could only seat 52 passengers, while their fuel consumption was distinctly poor when compared with Daimler COG5s. The TD6c was built to Birmingham specification and this was the only batch to be built. No 271 entered service on 11 March 1939 and lasted until April 1952 after spending almost all of its operational life at Hockley garage. The tramcar outlived the buses in Birmingham's service by a few months, being withdrawn when the Bristol Road routes closed on 5 July 1952. *H. B. Priestley*

Below In this 1937 scene car 144 is mounted on Brush Peckham trucks; it was one of 20 of the ex-Mountain & Gibson radial-trucked 71 Class that had been re-motored in 1934 with 40 hp motors. It was in good condition when due for withdrawal, and as it was fitted with the DK13A motors, it became one of 22 of the Class retained in reserve throughout the Second World War.

Hockley depot usually had a small allocation of older four-wheelers; these were used on short-working main-line duties and car 144 was one of 15 that were allocated to the depot at this time.

The tram stands alongside the Farley Clock. Completed in the year of Queen Victoria's Diamond Jubilee, it had been given to the town by Alderman Reuben Farley, whose name can be seen on the terracotta panel on the clock tower alongside the tram. He had been Mayor of West Bromwich five times and had donated the magnificent Elizabethan Oak house to the town. Just behind the clock can be seen a totally enclosed bogie car leaving for the town centre on the 75 service. *R. T. Wilson*

The Farley Clock not only marked the end of the 'Golden Mile' of West Bromwich High Street, but also the point at which the routes to Dudley diverged. To the right, cars 517 and 520 are on the 754 route, the former inbound and 520 travelling towards Wednesbury. Of the two cars on the track to the left of the clock, only the second tram, car 608, is working into Birmingham from Dudley on the 74 route. Car 548, on the 73 route, has turned after reversing at the cross-over at the clock tower.

This 1938 scene shows the 1876 Methodist church in the background. This survived until 1970 when, after several years as a warehouse, it was demolished because of future road widening that has now left the clock as an isolated traffic island. *W. A. Camwell*

Wednesbury route

From Carters Green the Wednesbury route dropped down to Black Lake, then climbed gently to Hill Top. Here, just prior to the First World War, South Staffordshire open-top car 42 passes Hill Top Primary School, with its two cupola bell-towers, at the Coles Lane junction. The tram is travelling towards the steep Holloway Bank and descent into Wednesbury.

Car 42 is one of the former Birmingham & Midland 'Aston' types built by the Brush Company in 1904, of which a number were purchased by the South Staffordshire Company in 1912. They were the same as the ex-CBT trams numbered 243-256, four of which became Birmingham Corporation 498-501. *D. R. Harvey collection*

About 70 years later Hill Top has retained some of its pre-1914 features. The width of the main A41 road has hardly changed from when South Staffs tramcar 42 was followed by a lone cyclist. The house on the right just before the Coles Lane traffic lights has lost its chimneys, but the frontage, with the two bay windows, is largely unaltered. Just visible through the trees is Hill Top Junior School, which had closed and was, in the summer of 1994, being demolished. *D. R. Harvey*

Left 'BIRMINGHAM TRAM IN HILL TOP MEETS HORSE HEAD ON!' On Holloway Bank on Friday 31 March 1939 Brush-built car 592 is seen going towards the Wednesbury terminus about three-quarters of a mile away. Struggling up the steep hill is a horse and cart and just at the crucial moment the horse's head has got into the photograph.

This section of the route had been notorious for the poor quality of the track, and after a threat was made by Birmingham to withdraw the service, the track was relaid in the mid-1930s by West Bromwich, which was responsible for its upkeep. Latterly this allowed for some spirited performances on the 75 service. *R. T. Wilson*

Middle left Car 565 is on Holloway Bank, on the 75 route, on 31 March 1939. The steep 'S' bend into the Tame Valley at Wednesbury had originally evolved to ease the climb out of the valley by horse-drawn vehicles.

Wednesbury had been one of the cornerstones around which the Industrial Revolution in the Black Country had been based. From being one of the world's most important iron-producing centres in the mid-18th century, Wednesbury had specialised in the making of steel tubes. This industry had been particularly badly hit in the Depression of the 1930s and unemployment in the town reached over 30 per cent. The cobbled main road and the slightly run-down nature of the houses on Holloway Bank reflect an air of previous prosperity that had been badly hit since the Great War. The houses survived into the 1970s and the tram continued in service until July 1953. *R. T. Wilson*

Below left When BCT took over the route to Wednesbury both Walsall Corporation and Wolverhampton District trams, as successors to the South Staffordshire Tramways, also terminated near the White Horse public house at the junction of Lower High Street with Holyhead Road. For about five years this was the only place in the West Midlands where three different operators of trams met.

Totally enclosed Brush car 613 is loading up with passengers opposite the public house, prior to returning to West Bromwich and Birmingham. Although by this date it was about eight years old, the tram, when compared to the Wolverhampton District tramcar, appears quite modern. The Company car was a Brush-built 'Aston' type four-wheeler that had originated with the Birmingham & Midland company.

In the foreground one track linking the West Bromwich line to the Darlaston section has been severed. When the South Staffordshire Company's lease expired on 31 March 1924 there were thoughts that Birmingham Corporation should operate the complete route to Bilston. After running a Hockley bogie car through to Darlaston, it was decided to terminate at Wednesbury because of the side-running overhead.

On the extreme right is an open-balconied Walsall Corporation four-wheeler from the 40-49 Class built by Brush in 1919. It was to have a life of only 14 years, unlike 613 which ran until it sustained collision damage in December 1952. The photograph was taken between September 1927, when the balcony of car 613 was enclosed, and September 1930, when the company trams were withdrawn. *Walsall Corporation*

BIRMINGHAM TRAMS 1933-53

Right On Saturday 25 March 1939, only one week before the abandonment of the tram service, car 514 stands at the White Horse pub in Wednesbury waiting to return to the city on the 75 route. The tram, one of the UEC-bodied, re-motored high-speed cars, was already 26 years old. It is in company with Walsall Corporation's Dennis 'Lance' bus 202 (FDH 863), which was less than one year old and is about to return to Walsall via Darlaston on the 37 route. The tram would outlive the nearly new bus by one year, as it was not withdrawn from service until Friday 4 July 1952 when the Bristol Road routes were closed. *A. N. H. Glover*

Dudley route

Middle right The Dudley route, after leaving Carters Green, passed through Swan Village, an area of heavy engineering and steel manufacturing dominated by the gas works, before reaching the Market Place at Great Bridge.

Great Bridge developed in the 1780s when the Ryder's Green branch of the Wednesbury to Birmingham canal was opened. The district had a further boost to its prosperity when the London & North Western Railway developed two interchange points with the canal at the Great Bridge Basin in the mid-19th century. These were some of the last canal/railway interchange points to remain, falling into disuse in the early 1960s.

The short-working to Great Bridge was numbered 76, but only one or two peak journeys and a couple after the last Dudley service at night were scheduled. Car 545 is a 74 service tram suitably posed for the photographer on 9 August 1938. The centre of Great Bridge was a triangle that leads today to the small bus station. In mid-1995 part of the A41 replacement road from the M5 at West Bromwich was opened, which relieved the junction of some of its traffic. *W. A. Camwell*

Right One of the problems encountered by the South Staffordshire Company Tramways was the height of the Ryland Aqueduct at Dudley Port, which precluded the operation of top-covered trams. The aqueduct, on the Birmingham Canal Navigation's New Main Line canal, had been opened on 2 April 1838. The canal was designed by Thomas Telford to replace the meanderings of the earlier James Brindley canal, which Telford had referred to as 'that Crooked Ditch'. It cut a swath through the industrial heartland of the Black Country from Birmingham to Wolverhampton.

It was only after Birmingham Corporation took over in April 1924 that it became possible to get its lower trams under the 16 ft 4¼ in bridge. The wiring was at the side of the road and the trolley was pushed wide and below the level of the roof of the tramcar. Here an unidentified bogie car slowly enters the damp gloom beneath the railway bridge and the Ryland Aqueduct in late March 1939.

All the Birmingham enclosed bogie double-deckers from 512 to 843 inclusive could pass underneath Dudley Port, but of the four-wheelers only the 301 and 401 Classes were low enough.

This 1939 view, although very dark, reveals that this is very near to the end of tramcar operation on the route. Just visible behind the tram is a West Bromwich Corporation MCCW-bodied Daimler COG5, possibly being used by the workmen alongside the tram painting white lines on the cobbles. These pre-date the two lines of studs that were later put in place. Drivers of double-deck buses had to keep clear of the space between the white lines and the kerb if they were to pass through the low arches safely. *P. Spencer*

Car 609 squeezes through the low bridge on its way from Dudley on 7 September 1938. Trams were subject to a 4 mph speed limit here because of the pointwork leading into the single-line section under both the aqueduct and the railway bridge and the slewed overhead, which took the trolley-pole wide of the tramcar to the western side of the arched bridges.

Only certain top-covered trams were allowed through Dudley Port and these carried a rectangular plate on the signal lamp rails, with the inscription: LOW BRIDGE CAR / SELLY OAK, ASTON / DUDLEY PORT. *W. A. Camwell*

Today virtually nothing remains from the previous view. The aqueduct was rebuilt with a flat span, while the railway bridge was rebuilt when the main line between Birmingham and Wolverhampton was electrified. The main road, the A461, has been widened to a dual-carriageway, while the balustrade of the aqueduct has railings with barge silhouettes cut into them. The height of the approaching lorry shows that the restrictions at Dudley Port no longer pose a problem to tall vehicles. So while that problem has gone, so have the trams! *D. R. Harvey*

Dudley Port was the name of the road as well as the district, and seen here climbing up Dudley Port towards Burnt Tree on the 74 route is Brush-built bogie car 617. It is Thursday 14 April 1938 and the tram, which is nearly full, has just overtaken a large Austin Twenty saloon, parked near to the Waggon & Horses, an Atkinson public house that occupied No 71, Dudley Port. Car 617 had been allocated to Hockley depot for most of its service life since it entered service in 1920, but would move to Selly Oak in April 1939. *H. B. Priestley*

BIRMINGHAM TRAMS 1933-53

The 74 route approached Dudley from Dudley Port and, on reaching Burnt Tree at Tividale, joined the former Birmingham & Midland Tramway line from Smethwick and Oldbury. An open-balconied 71 Class tram can be seen on this latter route climbing up the hill from Tividale, with the tower of the church on the skyline in this photograph taken on 6 September 1938. To the left of the tram can be seen a policeman who is on point duty at the New Birmingham Road crossing.

On the left, car 634 has climbed Burnt Tree and has also crossed the New Birmingham Road (A4123) or, as it is known locally, 'The Wolver'. The two routes and the New Birmingham Road made a grassy triangle, long since subsumed by the enlargement of this important road junction. *W. A. Camwell*

The end of the 9-mile journey to Dudley was just beyond Midland Red's garage, which is the building to the extreme left of the photograph and which had opened on 2 August 1929. Car 607, a Brush-built bogie car, waits at the terminus, ready to return to Birmingham on the 74 service on 23 October 1938. Immaculately turned out, the 18-year-old tram still retains the old 'Birmingham Corporation Tramways and Omnibus Dept.' legal lettering on its rocker panel, showing that it had not been repainted since the title was changed in November 1937. In the late 1930s it was quite common for the trams to have posters advertising local events on their fenders, in this case the Birmingham University Hospital Carnival Fair. *A. N. H. Glover*

The last tramcar to leave Dudley via West Bromwich was car 535, which ran back as far as Carters Green to be replaced by the ex-Radial four-wheel car 128 as illustrated earlier. Car 535 was at Moseley Road depot by the following Saturday.

The enthusiasts lean out of the top deck to be recorded for posterity as car 535 stands on the railway bridge at the bottom of Castle Hill for the last time. Although previous abandonments had occurred, the passing of the Handsworth routes somehow signalled the beginning of the end of the BCT tram system. Here was a largely relaid tramway, operated by the fastest trams in the fleet, but because of the expiry of the lease, which could have been renewed, the routes were closed.

After car 535 left Dudley, late on Saturday night 1 April 1939, only the 87 route remained to run into the Black Country via Smethwick and Oldbury to terminate in Dudley, and this used the older 71 class cars. *D. R. Harvey collection*

STECHFORD ROUTES

THE TRAM routes to Stechford developed as the city expanded to the east. The first route was opened on 24 November 1906 between High Street and Blake Lane, Bordesley Green, via Fazeley Street, and was the fourth Birmingham Corporation-operated service to be opened.

The trams left the original terminus in Albert Street, which marked the edge of the retail area of the city centre. The shop-lined streets quickly gave way to warehouses in Fazeley Street, but by the time the trams had passed beneath the LNWR railway bridge at New Canal Street, the landscape had become one of small factories and workshops. After crossing the Bordesley Wharf arm of the Warwick & Birmingham Canal and the River Rea, the route turned sharp left into Great Barr Street and climbed sharply over the same canal between the walls of the Great Western Railway's never-completed Duddeston viaduct.

The majority of Great Barr Street was single-track as far as Lawley Street; here the route curved to the right and climbed up Garrison Lane where the track was interlaced between Barwell Street and Gray Street as it went over the narrow Birmingham & Warwick Junction Canal bridge. This was almost immediately followed by a short single-line section over the Midland Railway's Camp Hill

line before continuing the three-quarters-of-a-mile climb to Tilton Road. The last section of Garrison Lane was used to park trams for the home games of Birmingham FC, whose St Andrews ground backed on to Tilton Road.

The line continued past rows of terraced houses until the junction with Bordesley Green was reached at the Atlas public house. It was here that the second route from the city, via Cattell Road, met the Garrison Lane route and both continued to the Blake Lane terminus through an area of Edwardian housing. This second service to Bordesley Green via Digbeth, Coventry Road and Cattell Road was introduced from High Street on 2 April 1913. A third route starting from Station Street was introduced at the same time, but this was unremunerative and was abandoned on 13 May 1913.

The new route began in High Street and until 1930 went down Carrs Lane to Moor Street. After this date the terminal loop was reversed and the cars left the Beehive Store in Albert Street, turning right into Moor Street along with the Moseley Road and Stratford Road services. In Moor Street the trams passed the Great Western Railway's terminus before turning into the Bull Ring opposite the Parish Church of St Martin and descending into Digbeth.

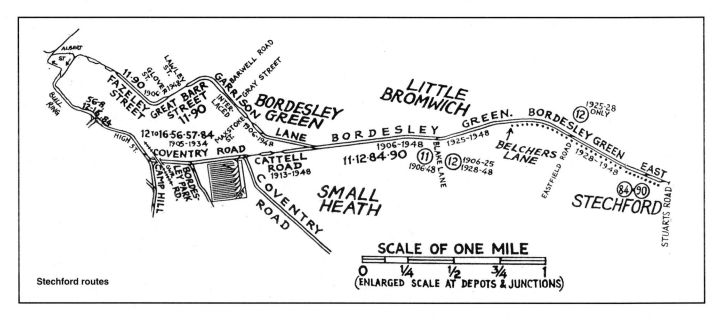

Stechford routes

The Digbeth area is the original site of Birmingham and was the medieval bridging point of the River Rea. By the turn of the century Digbeth had become the first small shopping centre out of the city centre, with narrow side roads leading into an area of small factories. The Moseley trams turned right into Rea Street while the Bordesley Green route carried on in company with the Stratford Road routes through industrial Deritend towards the Bordesley junction where Bordesley cars turned left under Bordesley railway bridge and into Coventry Road.

At the top of Kingston Hill the Bordesley trams passed Coventry Road (or Arthur Street) depot and the junction with Cattell Road at the Greenway Arms public house. The climb of Kingston Hill slightly flattened out at the south side of St Andrews football ground and the housing began to change from mid-19th-century back-to-backs and three-storeyed terraces to the later tunnel-back houses. At the eastern end of Cattell Road the route joined the Garrison Lane route.

In 1908 the Fazeley Street service was lettered 'B' on a black background while the Digbeth service was introduced as 'B' on a blue background. When route numbers were introduced in 1915 the service via Fazeley Street became 11 and the Deritend route was numbered 12.

The Deritend service was extended on Wednesday 4 November 1925 to Eastfield Road, partly on reserved track, to serve the council house development being constructed at Batchelor's Farm. Finally, on Tuesday 26 August 1928, a further extension along reserved track reached Stuarts Road, Stechford, the Deritend service being numbered 84 and the Fazeley Street route becoming the 90. This was the last major tram route extension on the BCT system.

The service was run initially by Brill-trucked, open-topped four-wheel cars, which were quickly supplemented by 71 Class Radial trams. After the conversion of the Coventry Road trams to trolleybuses in January 1934, the Brills were gradually transferred or withdrawn. In 1939 the 71 Class cars were to be withdrawn and were replaced on the Stechford routes by 301 Class cars, which worked the route until the final closure. Bogie cars were something of a rarity on Stechford's routes but the ex-CBT bogie cars 451 and 452 are known to have worked on the Bordesley Green service in open-top condition before their conversion to single-deck in 1917. One of the original abandonment plans had involved the early closure of Moseley Road's routes and the transfer of the 401 Class air- and oil-brake trams to Coventry Road, but the programme was altered and the proposed Stechford closures, intended for 1 April 1940, were shelved because of the war. The Stechford services were abandoned on Saturday 2 October 1948 when car 316 was the last tram back into the depot.

City Centre to Bordesley

Reminders of the recently ended Second World War could be seen for many years afterwards on the streets of Britain's towns and cities. Scenes such as this, taken on Saturday 31 May 1947, show members of the armed forces, in this case the Royal Air Force, walking past the Glenn Cafeteria in High Street. The Daimler COG5 bus turning into Albert Street on the 37 route has its rear dome and roof painted in the wartime khaki, while just visible beyond the sign for the News Theatre is a grey-painted 301 Class tram. The other member of the same open-balconied Class in this view is car 395, working on the 84 route. Little did anyone realise that this would be the only Birmingham tramcar to survive closure of the system six years later!

The Daimler COG5 bus coming down Bull Street shows the unhelpful destination blind CITY. To anyone who lived in Birmingham at this time, this meant that the bus had come from Kingstanding via Lozells following the 29 route, as this display was used in normal service for this route. It is passing Preedy's Corner; this large tobacconist shop occupied the corner site of Bull Street and Dale End. This bus is about to cross the tram tracks that enabled inbound cars from Dale End to turn into Martineau Street (see page 34 of Volume 1). *J. S. Webb*

Left On the last day of operation, Saturday 2 October 1948, a slightly unkempt car 327 waits next to the canopied loading stands outside S. Baylis's shop loading up before going to Stechford on the 84 route. The 52-seater UEC-bodied 40 hp four-wheeled tram, delivered in the spring of 1911, was to be broken up there in January 1949. It was one of 50 of the Class that received the wartime grey livery in 1942 and was repainted in the pre-war style in 1945. Beyond it is Leyland TTBD2 six-wheeled trolleybus 44 (OC 1144), which is leaving the shelters after loading up for the city boundary at Sheldon.

The track at the bottom of Albert Street had been abandoned earlier in the year because an unexploded wartime bomb was suspected near-by. The 90 route had previously terminated in Albert Street, but for several months had been truncated to Fazeley Street. This warehouse-bound street is to the right of the building in the distance above the roof of the Standard 8 car. *T. J. Edgington*

Left The lack of any shop window displays in the Beehive Store in Albert Street may reflect the early post-war period of shortages and rationing. By 1948, nine years without anything that was not controlled by Government austerity restrictions had made Birmingham, like many other cities, a grey, cheerless place.

For about 11 years Albert Street had been the only city terminus where all three modes of public transport could be seen together; trams, the Coventry Road trolleybuses and motor buses shared the same row of stops. Car 363 stands in front of an unidentified Leyland six-wheeled trolleybus and a Stratford Road-bound Daimler COG5. The tram, after a three-year sojourn at Coventry Road depot, would see out another two years' service elsewhere, to become one of the final 23 four-wheelers in the fleet. *J. S. Webb*

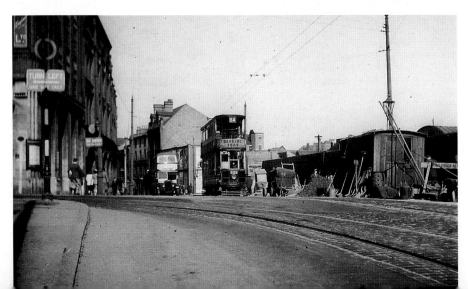

Below left After leaving the city terminus in Albert Street the trams turned right into Moor Street. They then climbed up the short hill to meet the inbound cars, whose tracks can be seen in the foreground turning into Carrs Lane at the Corner public house. Car 332, working the 84 route on 27 March 1948, is being followed by MCCW-bodied Daimler COG5 874 (BOP 874). This 1936-built bus is working on the 376 service to Hall Green; this followed the route of the former 17 tram route along Stratford Road, which had been abandoned on 5 January 1937 only five months after the bus had entered service. The bus's radiator is still painted black, a remnant of a wartime measure. Tram 332 was withdrawn on 2 October 1948 when the Stechford service closed, and was taken to Moseley Road where it was broken up in December of that year. *J. S. Webb*

BIRMINGHAM TRAMS 1933-53

Standing at the bus stop outside Nelson House, No 2 Moor Street, is car 354, working the 84 route via Digbeth to Stechford, with notices in its windows advising of the impending route abandonment. A small queue of intending passengers is already moving off the pavement, as in those days walking into the middle of the road to get on a tramcar was still the normal thing to do, for the other traffic would have posed little threat to their safety.

Although this tram would only remain in service for just over a year after the closure of the Stechford routes, it was to lose its pre-war livery in favour of the simplified 1946 style. Yet despite the tram's apparent need of a repaint, it had run for most of the wartime period painted all-over grey. Having left the stop, the trams travelled the few yards to the corner of Moor Street and the Bull Ring before turning left to descend the steep hill opposite the parish church of St Martin. *J. S. Webb*

Car 301 is seen during 1948 turning from Moor Street into the Bull Ring on its way out of the city on the 84 route. The first shop in the Bull Ring was shoe retailer Griffiths Allen, whose doorway was actually on the corner of Moor Street. No 14 next door was called Hobbies, a shop specialising in fretwork and balsa-wood models.

This area was badly damaged on 10 April 1941 when nearly everything from Oswald Bailey's Army and Navy Stores, which was on the opposite corner of Moor Street from Griffiths Allen, up the Bull Ring as far as High Street was destroyed. The parlous state of the buildings can be seen by the enormous wooden buttress placed against the premises of James Glover & Sons, agricultural engineers.

Despite its run-down condition, car 301 soldiered on in service at Washwood Heath and Moseley Road depots for another 12 months after the closure of the Stechford routes. *D. R. Harvey collection*

Car 358 has just passed the strangely designed Portland stone-faced frontage of Digbeth Police Station at the corner of Allison Street and Digbeth. It was built in 1911 with a clock-tower and cupola mounted on a mock Wren-style structure. On the extreme left is the Lightfoot Refrigeration Co Ltd's Ice Works, where the air-braking system from tramcar 802 was tested in September 1930 to ascertain its working characteristics in sub-zero temperatures. Such testing was done because of a discovery that the air-brake auto-valves on the 762 Class tended to freeze up.

On the left behind the tram and its following trolleybus are the shops that lined Digbeth towards the Civic Hall and Rea Street. All the remaining buildings to the right of Digbeth on the south side were demolished in connection with the dualling of the carriageway, and much of the site has been occupied since 1958 by Spencer House and the Midland Red coach station. *J. S. Webb*

Above Car 327 leaves the compulsory tram stop outside the Old Bull's Head public house and passes in front of the mock-Dutch frontage of the Digbeth Institute. The hexagonal stop sign for the Coventry Road trolley-buses can be seen above the tram stop plate. For many years the Stechford and Moseley Road services shared this pick-up point; the trams working on the latter route turned into Rea Street, which is to the right of the removal van that is overtaking the tramcar. At the time of the Stechford abandonment, on Saturday 2 October 1948, Coventry Road depot had allocated to it 39 trams of the 301 Class, and of these car 327, only at the depot since February 1945, was one of 22 cars not to see service again.

Digbeth had been the original route into the medieval settlement of Birmingham from the south, with a ford across the River Rea, a minor river fed by some 25 small brooks. A Norman Lord of the Manor created a dam some 500 yards downstream of the fording point to create a millpond, but this frequently caused the Rea valley to flood. The last bridge was built as recently as 1813, but by then the river had become a major obstacle to transport across the Digbeth area. In the latter part of the 19th century, the river was culverted into a brick-lined channel. Its presence today would hardly be noticed by the passer-by except for street names such as Rea Street and Floodgate Street, and the significance of this small valley to the development of Birmingham has been lost. *F. N. Lloyd Jones*

Above right Passing the Old Bull's Head and the renamed and refurbished Digbeth Institute is MCW 'Metrobus' 2227 (GOG 227W). The eastern side of

Digbeth remains largely as it was in tram days, although the road was made into a dual-carriageway in July 1955; this had been planned as long ago as 1935. But for the outbreak of the Second World War, the Stechford trams would have been replaced in 1940; had the plan been implemented the oldest surviving trams at that time would have been the open-balconied, four-wheel 301 Class, and most of the 100-strong batch would have gone fairly quickly. The proposed starting date for the widening of Digbeth and Deritend was a major consideration as to the date of the Stechford abandonment. In the event, both the original street pattern and some of the 301 Class survived into the 1950s! Digbeth and Deritend were amongst the most congested thoroughfares in the city, and by the time the Ministry of Transport had finally given permission for the road improvement scheme to be resumed, the trams had gone anyway! For once, the excuse that the trams were 'slow-moving and inflexible' had been overtaken by events. *D. R. Harvey*

Below left Car 348, complete with white-painted fenders, is re-poled on to the inbound tram overhead in Bradford Street. On Sunday 5 November 1939 it has been diverted to a temporary Hill Street terminus, which was being used because track repairs at the junction of Digbeth and Rea Street meant that the Stechford service was unable to reach Albert Street. The tram is travelling towards the distant Smithfield vegetable market in Moat Row. The market was built in 1883 and, when under construction, the remains of the medieval manor house of the de Bermingham family were discovered.

Just behind the tram on the overhead are the 500 volt dc electric feeder cables. The overhead was divided into half-mile sections, which enabled the current to be isolated if necessary within these sections.

This member of the 301 Class carries on its side panels the advertisement for the locally blended Typhoo Tea, though many a Brummie shopper referred to it as 'Typhoon Tea'! Car 348 was one of the first non-accident withdrawals of the 301 Class, being taken out of service in October 1944 as its body was in a poor state of repair. It was broken up at Sampson Road paint shop along with nine other trams that had been stored there during the war. *L. W. Perkins*

BIRMINGHAM TRAMS 1933-53

Right The rails of the curve that took the Moseley Road trams into Rea Street glint in the late afternoon sunshine as car 332, inbound from Stechford on the 84 route, begins to cross the junction and proceed into Digbeth. It is being followed by one of the 1940-built Leyland TB7 trolleybuses, 80 (FOK 80), with an MCCW 54-seat body. This will follow the tram through Digbeth and the Bull Ring to Albert Street.

Nearly all the buildings to the left of the Acocks Green-bound, almost new AEC 'Regent' III 0961 RT-type with a curiously proportioned Park Royal body, remain today, though everything to the right has long since disappeared. Advertisements at this time were not carried by either motor or trolleybuses, so of the three vehicles visible only the most elderly, tram 332, is carrying any sort of advertisement, in this case for the locally blended Barbers Teas. *J. S. Webb*

Middle right UEC top-covered car 120, built in 1906, was originally equipped with a Mountain & Gibson 8 ft 8 in radial truck, but was retrucked during the 1920s with a Brush Peckham P35 pendulum unit. It is on its way out of the city through Digbeth early in 1934, and is being passed in the opposite direction by one of the newly delivered Leyland TTBD2, MCCW-bodied trolleybuses, 57 (OC 1157), which had been introduced on 7 January of the same year. The second Leyland trolleybus behind car 120 is 17, the first of the Class; it is going to Yardley on the 92 route from Albert Street.

The trams shared Digbeth with the trolleybuses from 1934 until the Moseley Road abandonment, so the overhead layout was extremely complicated at this point. The positive wire was common to both trams and trolleybuses and was always the offside one where there were two.

The buildings behind the tram, which included the SPQR warehouse on the corner of Rea Street and Digbeth, dated from the early 1830s and was demolished prior to the Digbeth road-widening scheme of 1955. The legend 'SPQR' is Latin for 'Senatus Populusque Romanus', which means 'the Senate and the people of Rome'. Its relevance to a warehouse in the inner heartland of Birmingham is at first lost until its more corrupt latter day meaning is remembered - 'Small Profits and Quick Returns'. *D. R. Harvey collection*

Below The disappearing Daimler CVD6, 1784 (HOV 784), is working on the 44 bus route through Deritend on 27 May 1948, having entered service on the first of the same month. The UEC-bodied tram 388, built in 1911, is on an inbound 84 service and will be withdrawn at the end of 1949.

Deritend had been referred to in the 15th century as Deryatend, meaning Deer Gate End. This area had always been a centre for the back-street workshops that so typified the industrial entrepreneurialism of the citizens of Birmingham. Later growth replaced the small factories with larger, more imposing edifices, such as the Birds Custard factory, with its Art Nouveau frontage. Leyland TTBD2 trolleybus 35 (OC1135), working on the out-of-city 94 route is approaching this splendid piece of indulgent architecture.

To the right is the Thomas Haddon & Stokes screw and nut factory, which was built well back from the original alignment of Deritend so that the later 1950s road widening could take place. Today the Birds Devonshire Works remains, although it was vacated by Birds in the 1970s; after leading a somewhat charmed life it is being converted into The Custard Factory, a centre for arts and entertainment. Ironically, the newer Thomas Haddon & Stokes factory was demolished in the 1980s and the western side of Deritend is now occupied by a series of large car showrooms. *J. S. Webb*

Below Deritend lay on the original road to Coventry, Stratford and Warwick, and this medieval route pattern survives today as the main A45, A34 and A41 roads respectively. The industrial expansion of Birmingham across the flood plain of the Rea valley was relentless, and only a few architectural gems survived the encroaching 19th-century factories.

One of these survivors of the pre-industrial landscape is the Old Crown Inn. This timber-framed public house in part dates from 1368, though a good deal of it belongs to the 16th century. Built as mansion house, it became an inn about 1700, and its jettied frontage masks a rebuilding that took place in 1862.

Tram 311, working the 84 route, passes the inn on its way out of the city to Bordesley in 1948. This tram would be withdrawn after the Stechford closure later the same year. *J. S. Webb*

Beyond the Old Crown Inn, the 84 route continued to climb out of the valley of the Rea until it reached Adderley Street. Here the gradient flattened until the junction of Coventry Road and Camp Hill was reached. Car 327 passes the Rainbow public house at the corner of Adderley Street on 27 March 1948 when working the 84 route. Even before redevelopment enlarged the carriageway, High Street, Bordesley, was a fairly wide road.

Although the trams shared Deritend with both trolleybuses and buses, in this scene the only other Birmingham City Transport vehicles are pre-war Daimler COG5 double-deckers, including the city-bound 1089 (CVP 189), which is on the 44 route from Acocks Green.

Adderley Street led beneath the Great Western Railway's bridges to Liverpool Street garage, which operated some 150 buses. It was opened in September 1936 and operated on the Inner Circle bus route as well as those to the outlying suburbs in the east of the city such as Yardley, Garretts Green and Kitts Green. *J. S. Webb*

Car 337 has just turned from Coventry Road into High Street, Bordesley, working on an inbound 84 service to Albert Street.

Passing in the opposite direction and about to turn into Coventry Road and pass beneath Bordesley railway bridge is one of the six-wheeled 17-66 Class of Leyland TTBD2 trolleybuses *en route* to Sheldon.

The tram is only about half full, but at least two hardy travellers are sitting in the open front balcony. Car 337, along with ten others of the Class, had been withdrawn in May 1940 to form part of the emergency reserve fleet. With trams being damaged in air-raids, car 337 was restored to operational condition in April 1941 along with the other 301 Class cars and was painted in wartime grey livery in March 1943; it was repainted back into normal livery in April 1948. Car 337 survived the Stechford closure, and was finally broken up at Moseley Road in October 1949. *C. W. Routh*

At the same spot is similar UEC-bodied tram 309, which has just turned out of Coventry Road after negotiating Bordesley railway bridge and will leave the comparative security of the small traffic triangle and cross the bottom of Camp Hill into High Street, Bordesley.

An almost new Daimler CVD6 descends Camp Hill from the direction of Stratford Road. Just above the bus can faintly be seen the Georgian perpendicular-styled Holy Trinity church dating from 1822, with its twin octagonal angle turrets. The corner of Coventry Road and Camp Hill was occupied by a slightly newer group of premises, which included R. & D. Haddon, whose upholstery and furniture shop is seen immediately to the right of the tram; in later years these premises were occupied by a tattoo artist! Just around the corner, in Camp Hill, was a genuine Brummie cafe, whose bacon sandwiches supplied the workers of the Dowding & Mills electrical motor repair factory with splendid sustenance and whose tea was alleged to bend spoons! *Newman College*

Coventry Road

Right The railway bridge at Bordesley carried the Great Western Railway main line to the south of Birmingham. This route had been authorised to the Birmingham & Oxford Junction Railway, but the company was absorbed by the GWR in August 1848, and the line was finally opened on 30 September 1852. Intermediate stations were constructed according to demand, that at Bordesley opening in June 1855. This was at the end of a long viaduct section that ran from the Moor Street tunnel across the Rea valley to approach ground level again at Bordesley bridge as it crossed Coventry Road.

The bridge, carrying an advertisement for Maudslay lorries and buses, is seen here with car 308 speeding beneath it from the Camp Hill junction towards the distant Watery Lane junction where the trolleybuses are apparently congregating. Just above them can just be seen Kingston Hill, leading towards the depot. *W. J. Haynes*

Middle right The compulsory tram stop at the bottom of Kingston Hill, on Coventry Road opposite Bordesley Park Road, was shared with one for trolleybuses, whose hexagonal stop sign can also be seen on the first traction pole on the left. UEC-built car 332 starts the climb up Kingston Hill, Coventry Road, on 27 March 1948. It is passing on the left the paper mill of J. & W. Mitchell Ltd, and to the right the rows of tall-chimneyed early Victorian terraced housing. This is where the 22 service to Bolton Road turned off Coventry Road on the unremunerative service into Small Heath. At the top of the hill, rising almost church-like, is the imposing west end of Coventry Road (or Arthur Street) depot, where the Stechford trams were based.

This view also shows the difference in the pattern of the road setts, quite clearly demarcating that area for which the Tramways Department was responsible, the remainder of the carriageway being maintained by the Public Works Department. *J. S. Webb*

Below right The somewhat uncompromising frontal aspect of totally enclosed four-wheeler tram 342 is revealed in this view in Kingston Hill, Coventry Road. The 'Armoured Car', as the tram was nicknamed, waits at the compulsory stop on the inbound line, just short of the junction with Bordesley Park Road. The Board of Trade would not officially sanction totally enclosed 3 ft 6 in gauge, four-wheeled double-deckers. However, both Birmingham and Walsall Corporations managed to overcome the objection by temporarily licensing their 'experimental' trams. The two converted Birmingham tramcars ran for nearly 30 years in their enclosed balcony form without any mishaps. It was a pity that it was not possible to enclose the rest of the 301-360 Class and the slightly longer 361 and 401 Classes. These Classes represented some of the last traditionally designed, pre-First World War four-wheel trams.

The early Victorian terraces were by this time becoming, as was much of the inner city area, somewhat run-down. Yet within the city there were houses with communal water-pipes and outside lavatories that were a more obvious priority for demolition and redevelopment. These houses in Coventry Road survived well into the **1970s**. *T. J. Edgington*

Left Car 308 climbs Kingston Hill in company with a Standard Eight convertible, two trolleybuses and what appears to be a Morris 'Isis' dating from about 1931. The narrowness of the oppressive Victorian streets at this point was rather incongruously replaced from just above Bordesley Park Road by one of the few pre-Second World War housing schemes to be developed in the inner city area to replace slum property. Constructed in 1937, this scheme was intended to be a model for further developments, which were never implemented because of the outbreak of war; 98 two- and three-storey maisonettes were constructed, each having a sun balcony, and they can be seen behind the wide grassed open space to the right. The imposing wall of the Victorian Bordesley Paper Works only emphasises the brief change in land use along this stretch of Coventry Road, before the Kingston Cinema and the tram depot were reached. *F. N. Lloyd Jones*

Middle left The arched windows of the tram depot stand imposingly behind UEC 40 hp car 377. Variously known as Arthur Street and Coventry Road, the depot was opened on 24 November 1906. With the opening of the Bolton Road route and joint working along Coventry Road with the CBT from 1 January 1907, the number of trams occupying the depot increased considerably, as all the Stratford Road services were also operated from here until Highgate Road depot was opened on 25 November 1913. The depot usually had an allocation of about 95 trams until the closure of the Coventry Road tram routes (services 15 and 16) in 1934.

Car 377 is working the city-bound 84 route in this 1948 view. After the closure of the Stechford routes, it would continue to work, after being repainted in the modified 1946 livery, until the final operation of four-wheeler trams in the city at the end of October 1950. Three workmen are getting a lift on the back of the lorry, rather than catch the tram, and are hanging on as the lorry bumps over the cobbles. *R. T. Wilson*

Below left The interior of Coventry Road/Arthur Street depot on 18 March 1939 shows five of the 71-220 Class of open-balconied, UEC-built, ex-Mountain & Gibson Radial trams, constructed in 1906 and 1907. Cars 168, 174 and 109 had been retrucked in the 1920s with Brush Peckham P35 trucks, while cars 125 and 184 had an older Brush truck and a UEC 7 ft 6 in truck respectively. Cars 168, 174 and 184 were soon to be withdrawn, while cars 109 and 125 moved to Rosebery Street.

By the end of the first week of April, most of the 71 Class cars, which had been the mainstay of Coventry Road's services since it had opened, had gone. They were replaced by the lower and slightly more modern 301 Class, which had also been built by UEC but in this case in 1911.

With its maximum capacity of 106 cars Coventry Road was one of the largest depots on the Birmingham system, and by this time its allocation was around 45 trams to operate on the Stechford routes. The Coventry Road trolleybuses, one of which is just visible between cars 109 and 184, had shared the accommodation since January 1934 on the conversion of that route from trams. Gradually the allocation of trams for the Stechford services declined so that by the abandonment on 2 October 1948 there were only 37 of the 301 Class left in service at Coventry Road depot. *W. A. Camwell*

With two boys leaning over the balcony rails looking at the unloading and loading passengers, car 375 stands at the junction of Cattell Road and Coventry Road. Until 1934 the 'main-line' Coventry Road tram tracks occupied the large open space of cobbles in the foreground, but by 1948, when this photograph was taken, the Stechford trams had been the only railed occupants of the Coventry Road for some 14 years. The 84 route and its short-working, the 12 route to Bordesley Green, went straight on up the hill of Cattell Road, while the trolleybuses turned right along the flatter part of the A45 main road and on through Small Heath.

This stop served the Victorian-built shopping centre that had grown up just east of the tram depot. It is almost in the shadow of Birmingham City FC's St Andrews ground, which had been opened in 1906 at the same time that the club changed its name from Small Heath Athletic FC.

This part of Bordesley was an intensively quarried site of about 100 acres. It had on it a maximum of eight brickworks, which utilised the local red clay. St Andrews football ground occupies the site of one of these brickworks. *J. S. Webb*

This view of the mid-Victorian shopping centre clustered around the Coventry Road-Cattell Road junction is looking out of the city. The almost new Walsall-registered Ford Anglia in the foreground, which belonged to the photographer, dates this busy scene to 1948. Coventry Road took the right-hand curve in front of the Greenway Arms public house. Just visible behind the approaching tramcar, 327, is one of Midland Red's brand-new JHA-registered AEC 'Regent' IIs working on the 159 route to Meriden and Coventry. Jumping off the tram outside Coventry Road depot are two platform staff about to start their duties. The depot also housed the entire trolleybus fleet, which at that time numbered 74 vehicles. With both trams and trolleybuses there was an extremely complicated overhead wiring arrangement outside the depot entrance. *J. S. Webb*

Car 314 descends Cattell Road and enters the double-tracked section at the junction with Coventry Road. Car 368, basically similar but built 6 inches longer, waits for the city-bound 314 to enter the double track section before moving into Cattell Road which was single-track with one passing loop until the junction with the 90 route trams at Garrison Lane was reached.

This view, taken on Wednesday 29 September 1948, reveals something of the complex nature of combining tram and trolleybus overhead. The trolleybuses, turning into Coventry Road on the right and sharing with the trams the positive overhead wire, actuated a device that moved the frog on the positive overhead wire, so enabling the trolleybuses to turn into Coventry Road. This meant that the Stechford trams always had access into Cattell Road. As there were no road markings at this junction, to assist trolleybus drivers in foggy weather there was a string of small lights on the overhead, which are just visible around the curve of Coventry Road in front of the Greenway Arms. *W. A. Camwell*

Left The passing loop in Cattell Road was on the bend between Tilton Road and Templefield Street. In this September 1948 view, car 312 (on the left), on its way out of city going towards Bordesley Green, passes car 332 on the 84 route. Both of these trams were broken up at Moseley Road depot by George Cohen & Son after the closure of the Stechford services.

The three-storeyed back-to-back houses in Cattell Road dated from the 1860s. These grim houses with their blue-bricked courtyards had reached their outer limit of growth, and gradually began to give way to the later smaller, but more sanitary, post-1870 Housing Act developments that are seen to the left of the photograph.

The Bordesley Green service had been opened via Deritend as far as Blake Lane on 2 April 1913 as route 'B'; it later became the 12 route and joined the 11 service at the Atlas public house. *J. S. Webb*

Below Standing at the Templefield Street end of the passing loop in Cattell Road is UEC four-wheel car 321. The remnants of the wartime markings can be seen on the traction-poles; these white bands were painted on all street furniture to make them more visible in the blackout.

The general run-down nature of the area was to remain for over 20 years after the last Stechford trams had rattled their way into history on Saturday 2 October 1948. The clanking of the trams echoing between the confines of the houses along Cattell Road were then replaced by the gentler tones of the Daimler CVD6s of the 1756-1843 Classes on the new 54 bus service. These buses were amongst the quietest and the most refined of all the early post-war Birmingham buses. Car 321 was to become one of the last of the 301 Class to remain in service, not being withdrawn until October 1950, by which time it had been repainted in the simplified 1948-style livery. *J. S. Webb*

City Centre to Garrison Lane

The other 'arm' of the Bordesley route also started from Albert Street, but ran to Bordesley Green via the industrial back streets of Fazeley Street and Garrison Lane. In the summer of 1948 the connection between the 84 route, which turned into Moor Street, and the 90 route, which went straight on into Fazeley Street, was cut when an unexploded bomb was suspected to be buried just south of the connection. The 90 route was cut back to the top of Fazeley Street, which meant that the service cars stopped in a terminal stub just below the normal final passing loop before reaching Albert Street.

Car 314 waits at the temporary terminus in mid-September 1948, with its trolley-pole turned before rumbling through the cobbled streets amongst the tall warehouses that dominated this area just outside the shopping streets of the city centre. *J. S. Webb*

BIRMINGHAM TRAMS 1933-53

Right The curtailment of the 90 service to Seymour Street, just north of the Park Street junction, was only going to be temporary, but the track was never restored before the final abandonment on 2 October 1948. Albert Street, which is behind the photographer, had been built as a 'new and commodious' half-mile-long 'railway boulevard', which had been cut as part of the street commissioners' plans to link the then newly opened Curzon Street railway station with the town centre. It was opened in 1851, some 14 years after the station was opened, but because of problems over land ownership and the demolition of old properties, the scheme was only completed in 1862, by which time Curzon Street station had long since been closed and replaced by the LNWR's New Street station in the middle of the town. Thus the extension of the town centre to the south never came into being and the impressive shops and warehouses of Albert Street gradually petered out into the small factories and workshops that had already developed in the Fazeley Street area amongst which car 380 stands.

This UEC 52-seat four-wheeler stands at the temporary city terminus of the 11 and 90 routes, its platform staff looking curiously at the photographer. This tram had come to Coventry Road depot in April 1939 to replace the earlier 71 Class cars that were being withdrawn. It survived the Stechford closure, but was stored in Kyotts Lake Road Works after September 1949 until finally broken up in February 1950. *R. T. Wilson*

Middle right Standing beneath the gloom of Fazeley Street railway bridge are cars 344 and 354, working on the inbound and outbound 90 route respectively. Car 344 has another 200 yards or so to reach its terminus, just visible in the distance at the bottom of Albert Street. Car 354 is about to cross New Canal Street, to the right of the photograph, on its way out of the city.

Along New Canal Street lies Birmingham's first railway station at Curzon Street. This was built by the London & Birmingham Railway to the symmetrical design of a London architect, one Philip Hardwick. The design had four 45-feet-high Ionic-capitalled columns in a smaller version of Euston station's propylaeum design, and was available for the first through trains to London on 17 September 1838. This important architectural and transport gem was to lead a charmed life; it was closed to regular passenger services on 1 July 1854 and finally closed for holiday excursion traffic on 22 May 1893. It then became solely a goods station, after the new central station in Birmingham, New Street, was formally opened on 1 June 1854. The L&B's successor, the London & North Western Railway, reached New Street by an that which passed over the bridge in the photograph. *F. N. Lloyd Jones*

Right The 11 tram service was the original one to Bordesley Green, terminating at Blake Lane, which virtually marked the limit of housing development in the east of the city. When the route was opened in November 1906 it was given the route letter 'B', and subsequently became a short-working of the Stechford service. On Friday 4 August 1939 car 400 is in Fazeley Street at the Bordesley basin branch bridge of the Birmingham Canal Navigation, which had opened in 1799. It is an area of canal architecture that is almost hidden from view and whose value today as a piece of architectural heritage has only recently been appreciated.

The tramcar is carrying a good rush-hour load, although, unlike the fol-

lowing car 302 on the 90 route, its passengers have not spilled over on to the balconies. It is not carrying advertisements, which although not uncommon, does highlight the superb condition in which Birmingham's tramcar fleet was kept. It is passing a hoarding advertising Ascot gas water heaters, which would give hot water 'in a second'. *L. W. Perkins*

Left At the end of Fazeley Street the outbound trams turned left into Great Barr Street at the Forge Tavern. The ornate Victorian pub lantern must have been almost within touching distance of the open balcony of the trams as they squealed around the tight curve. The public house itself survives today as a Marston's hostelry, although its lamp has disappeared.

Car 314, seen in this early post-war view on the 90 route, turns the tight corner as a bus crew leave the tram to walk to the nearby Liverpool Street bus garage, to the right of the junction only about 200 yards away. Ironically, the Stechford trams were the most regular form of transport to the garage as the passing City Circle 19 bus service only ran in the peak periods by this time. *D. R. Harvey collection*

Right Car 321 descends from the Warwick & Birmingham Canal bridge in Great Barr Street, working the city-bound 90 route from Stechford. As in the previous photograph, BCT platform staff have left the tram to walk around the corner into Liverpool Street to the nearby bus garage. The tram will take the curve in the foreground past the Forge Tavern and turn into Fazeley Street.

Among the 22 advertisements on the Sheffield's hoarding behind the splendidly ornate wrought-iron urinal, one extols the virtues of Oxydol, the washing powder that 'Keeps coloureds brighter', and another OXO cubes, a drink that the chubby-cheeked little boy appears to be enduring rather than enjoying.

The advertisement above the urinal which reads 'I failed England' in fact states that 'the industries of Birmingham are vital for England's recovery' and that 'Industry looks to us'. As the city of 'A Thousand and One Trades', Birmingham had hundreds of small workshops in the Digbeth area on which Birmingham's industrial reputation had been based since the middle of the previous century. Metal-bashing trades, turning and fabricating all took place in this part of the city and had contributed towards the recently completed war effort. By 1947, with rationing and the vital need to export of paramount importance, these advertisements were another reminder to the Brummie worker that yet more was required! One can only surmise what the reaction might have been around the workshops of Digbeth! *R. T. Wilson*

Right The same view taken in August 1993 shows that very little has changed. The urinal, like the Forge Tavern opposite, has lost its lamp, and the number of advertisements has been drastically reduced to just two, one for Royal cigarettes and the second for the film *Mario Bros*, which is partly obscured by 2484, POG 484Y, a 1984 MCW Metrobus II DR102/27 working the 97 route from Chelmsley Wood.

For the first time the buttress of the partly dismantled 1,100-yard Duddeston railway viaduct can be seen above the bus, its blue brickwork exposed by the removal of the huge hoarding.

This viaduct was built by the Great Western Railway in order to comply with the original 1846 Act of Parliament that required that the proposed broad gauge line to Oxford should start from a junction close to the London & North Western Railway's Curzon Street station, which would also serve as the joint terminus for both companies. The irony was that by the time the GWR had reached the boundary of the LNWR land in February 1853 the LNWR had extended its line to the New Street terminus and made any junction with the GWR quite impossible. The station at Curzon Street was also closed.

Neither company had wanted the connection, but the GWR was forced to make the viaduct as a condition of working its main line. What the LNWR had done was to prevent the GWR from gaining access directly to the Stour Valley line and Wolverhampton over its lines, and in the process had used up a considerable amount of GWR capital. The remains stand as a silent, trainless monument to the often preposterous Victorian power struggles that took place during the period of railway mania. *D. R. Harvey*

BIRMINGHAM TRAMS 1933-53

Right Seeming to leap over the canal bridge in Great Barr Street is car 388, a late 1911 example of the UEC-built Class of trams. This car looks in need of a repaint, but deceptively this repaint in the pre-war livery was done in 1945 to replace a wartime grey livery, but using inferior wartime paint.

The tram is mounted on UEC's own design of 'flexible-axle' swing-yoke 7 ft 6 in wheelbase trucks, which were designed to give the truck a certain amount of movement without the traumas that had occurred with the 71 Class cars' 8 ft 6 in wheelbase Mountain & Gibson radial trucks. However, problems with the UEC trucks occurred fairly quickly and they were made rigid within a few years of entering service. With the tight curve at the Forge public house having only just been negotiated and the steep climb up to the crest of the canal bridge, it is not surprising that the driver's speed regulations officially limited this section of route between Fazeley Street and Montague Street to 4 mph. The driver of 388 is obviously not obeying this rule, but the head-scarfed woman, who is striding purposefully towards Glover Street, looks as if she might be trying to outpace the tramcar! *F. N. Lloyd Jones*

Below The cloth-capped driver of the 1937-registered Ford Ten 7W stops at the junction of Montague Street and Great Barr Street at the Atkinsons-owned Minerva public house. He is waiting for recently repainted tramcar 336 to enter the double section of track on its inward journey into the city from Stechford on the 90 route. The tram is carrying the advertisement for the Horsefair-based Austin car dealers Evans & Kitchen Ltd, but there is not one example of that local car manufacturer's products in this view. Evans & Kitchen were also the main franchise holders for Morrison Electricars, and makers of battery-electric vehicles such as milk floats and bread vans. The tram is being followed by a series E Morris Eight and has just passed a well-laden Morris Commercial 2-ton lorry. The results of wartime bombing can be clearly seen; the derelict site was soon to be occupied by a new factory for the Canning group of electroplaters, while on the traction poles are faded reminders of the wartime white stripes. *W. A. Camwell*

Left Near to the Lawley Street junction with Great Barr Street, BRCW-bodied Daimler COG5 bus 156 (EOG 156), built in 1938, is seen returning to Liverpool Street garage after working on a Villa Park Football Special. It is the last day of the Stechford trams and Aston Villa had just beaten Sheffield United 4-3. The bus is about to overtake open-balconied four-wheeler car 314, which is unloading passengers at the Lawley Street stop. Although the clock tower appears to be above the low-rise building on the corner of Ivy Lane and Great Barr Street, it belongs to the Wrights Ropes factory, whose chimney is visible on the skyline.

The tram, looking a little less smart than in the earlier photograph at the Forge Tavern, had been moved to Coventry Road depot on 20 September 1948 from Miller Street depot. This was necessary as in the last month of operation of the Stechford routes those members of the 301 Class that were in good condition and were allocated to Coventry Road depot were replaced by similar trams that were due for withdrawal. The trams that left Coventry Road for further service went to Washwood Heath, Miller Street or Witton; 314 was broken up at Moseley Road in January 1949. *J. S. Webb*

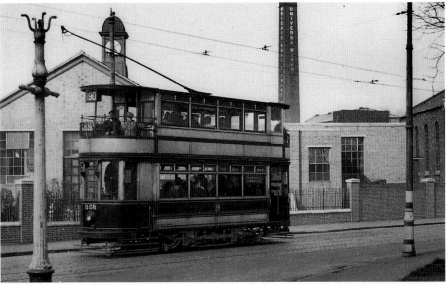

Left The old gas street light has been replaced in this 1948 view, as a fairly full car 358 passes it and the factory of a press tool manufacturer at the bottom of Garrison Lane. Behind the camera is a small recreation ground that had been used by the Transport Department during the war as a dispersal site for buses from Liverpool Street depot.

It was here in April 1941 that the late Fred Lloyd, whose photographs appear in Volume 1, and S. C. Miller drove 1133 (CVP 233), a 1937 Daimler COG5, which had caught fire having been hit by an incendiary bomb, away from the rest of the parked buses. Both men received the British Empire Medal for this act of bravery.

The Wrights Ropes Ltd factory chimney in Garrison Street can be seen in the background. Wrights made wire ropes, hawsers, twine and rope and were typical of the many small factories that existed in this area of Bordesley, though most were not graced with such a large chimney! *R. T. Wilson*

Below left The little boy in the pram leans inquisitively forward at the photographer while his big sister lolls disinterestedly over the handles of the pram and his mother fusses with them and the pram. They are passing the Garrison Lane recreation park, opened in 1912 to replace slum housing; it was a small lung of greenery amidst the factories and depressing Victorian houses of Bordesley. A small row of 1850s three-storeyed houses can be seen just behind tramcar 308, which is passing Garrison Lane Infants School.

The tram is about to negotiate a section of track that has had its stone setts dug up and the roadway between the rails excavated; it will move very slowly over the road works. Perhaps the little boy in the pram might be distracted from the camera by the noise of the passing tram. *J. S. Webb*

Right The planned road pattern of the 1870s housing in the Bordesley area rather belied the wide variation in housing styles in the area and the hilly landscape that was crossed by both canal and railway routes. The Acorn Inn in Barwell Road stands near some older Victorian housing opposite the descending tramcar. The houses beyond the cafe on the corner of Wolseley Street with their brick-embellished eave pediments and bay windows are more typical of the later buildings further along the route in Bordesley Green.

Car 322 is working inbound to the city on the 90 route, away from Birmingham City's St Andrews ground towards which numerous groups of boys and men are walking. It is Saturday 25 August 1948 and Birmingham City are playing Middlesbrough, a game that will end in a goalless draw.

The tramcar is on a section of interlaced track over the Birmingham & Warwick Junction

Canal bridge. This canal was one of the last to be built in the Birmingham area, opened on 14 February 1844. It linked Bordesley and the Warwick & Birmingham Canal with the Tame Valley and Fazeley Canals at Salford Bridge; this was done so that the congested canals of central Birmingham could be bypassed. Interlaced tram track was used sparingly in Birmingham, usually where there was insufficient clearance over bridges and through narrow thoroughfares. The two pairs of track retained their identity, but by running the two tracks in a road space little wider than just one track, enough space was left for other road traffic - in this case a solitary motor cycle! *W. A. Camwell*

Below Car 363 starts to move away from the compulsory tram stop in Garrison Lane at Maxstoke Street, and will shortly enter the eastern end of the interlaced double track section on its way towards the city. The descent of Garrison Lane towards Great Barr Street was subject to a 10 mph speed limit, although it was rarely observed by the time this view was taken.

On this quiet, gloomy Friday 22 August 1947, the lights are switched on in the Minerva Vaults public house. The young woman has just got off the tram, but needs only the most cursory of glances before crossing the road

as there is no vehicular traffic at all. Behind her is the curiously roofed building that served as offices for the adjoining and older factory premises. The tram carries the unusual 'Make a Note' advertisement for Bradshaws of Cregoe Street. They were not musical instrument suppliers, as might be thought, but ladies', gentlemen's and children's outfitters.

Car 363 was placed in store for over a year in 1940-41, but was returned to service and was among the last 301 Class cars to be withdrawn on the closure of Washwood Heath depot on 1 October 1950. *J. S. Webb*

Below Further east along Garrison Lane, the tram track became single line over the ex-Birmingham & Gloucester Railway's 1841-built line, the original line into Curzon Street from the south-west. Car 388, again one of the ubiquitous 301 Class, is just about to cross the railway bridge and start the steeper descent of Garrison Lane towards the River Rea valley, working on the 90 route towards the city. The pedestrians are walking on the only side of the bridge that has a pavement.

The houses just visible in the photograph were built in the 1860s, but those beyond Sydney Street, which was just out of the frame on the right, were of a later design and marked the start of the next ring of Victorian urban housing on Garrison Lane. *F. N. Lloyd Jones*

Above Once beyond the railway bridge and Sydney Road, the trams climbed up Garrison Lane on an increasingly steep gradient. Standing at the Venetia Road stop is car 344, and alongside it are various styles of late-19th-century terraced houses.

Opposite the tram can be seen East Holme, the middle of the three tiny cul-de-sacs (North and South are the other two) that ran off Garrison Lane. This small piece of land behind St Andrews football ground contained some of Birmingham's first experimental three-storey blocks of municipal flats. Designed in 1927 by D. H. Davies, the City Engineer's Housing Architect, there were 180 units in all, arranged around four cul-de-sacs (the fourth, West Holme, is off St Andrews Street). The flats were built with distinctive Dutch-style mansard roofs and included bathrooms and gas boilers; when opened, the Council rent for each flat was 8s 0½d. They were regarded as being so luxurious that they were nicknamed 'The Mansions'.

Birmingham's sub-standard houses in the inner areas at this time still accommodated nearly 200,000 people, but the success of the outer area housing schemes in Washwood Heath, Kingstanding, Erdington and Little Bromwich made the City Council reluctant to change from the formula of 12 houses per acre, which had proved so successful on the edge of the city. As a result very few flats were constructed before the Second World War and inner area redevelopment had to wait until the Central Development Area schemes of the 1950s. *F. N. Lloyd Jones*

Below The conductor, with his ticket punch and leather money bag, stands alongside car 125. This former Mountain & Gibson 8 ft 6 in Radial-trucked tram had been built in 1906 and had been fitted with a Brush 8 ft 6 in truck as early as 1909. It had also been re-motored from Dick, Kerr DK6A 35 hp motors to the more lively Dick, Kerr DK13A 40 hp ones in 1934. Despite this electrical upgrading and being re-vestibuled in the late 1920s and fitted with transverse seats, by the time this photograph was taken in Garrison Lane, opposite the flats, on Saturday 29 April 1939, the car was redundant. The closure of the Hockley routes, just four weeks earlier, had led to a surplus of bogie cars and the knock-on effect was that the 301 Class cars displaced from depots such as Selly Oak were transferred to Coventry Road to operate the Stechford services. The 71 Class cars were by this time surplus to requirements as they were no longer considered to be the 'workhorse' of the system, as had been the case for their first 20 years of service. They were restricted on the grounds of height, being 16 ft ½ in high to the trolley plank, whereas the 301 Class were 15 ft 7½ in and therefore could pass under any of the bridges on the system.

Car 125 would, within a few days, leave Coventry Road depot for Rosebery Street where it would remain until put into store for the duration of the war along with 21 others of the Class. For the benefit of the photographer, the destination blind has been wound round to show the 57 route; this Coventry Road service had been abandoned in 1934 when the route had been converted to trolleybus operation. *L. W. Perkins*

Right Car 373 descends Garrison Lane early in 1948 having passed the Tilton Road crossroads and the Royal George public house. It is passing South Holme, one of the three cul-de-sacs described opposite. After years of neglect, the flats were renovated by a housing trust in 1994 and have been incorporated into the Bordesley Village housing scheme that has regenerated the whole of this part of inner Birmingham. A whole swathe of this part of the city has been named Heartlands and slowly the derelict land and old factory sites are being replaced with new housing in adventurous settings such as alongside the canals.

Hardly the same could be said of the houses to the right of the tram. Although considerably better than the one block of back-to-backs just above the South Holme entrance, the 1870s terraces were in need of renovation even at this time, yet they were to remain occupied well into the 1970s before succumbing to road widening. The whole area from Venetia Road to Tilton Road was subsequently redeveloped, although not for housing; numerous small factory units and a few car scrap dealers have totally changed the urban landscape. *R. T. Wilson*

Right Less than one week before Neville Chamberlain returned from meeting the German Reichschancellor, Adolf Hitler, at Munich, Birmingham City were playing Preston North End at home in a First Division game on Saturday 24 September 1938. Car 179 brings up the rear in a line of 11 tramcars, with cars 158, 142 and 198 in front of it waiting for the emerging crowds to leave St Andrews and to take them by way of the 90 route back to the city.

All of these trams were members of the 71 Class. These had been built with unvestibuled bodies by the United Electric Car Co Ltd of Preston with a 52-seat capacity. They were originally mounted on Mountain & Gibson 8 ft 6 in Radial trucks, which were supposed to have the characteristics of a bogie car in that the individual axles could turn on a curve. Unfortunately, with wear, road dust and grit, the radial trucks often failed to return to their normal position and eventually they had to be locked up. Car 179 was fitted with a Brush-built Peckham P35 truck in October 1925 and ran with this until withdrawal in 1939.

The home fans coming out of the ground on that Saturday afternoon were not going to enjoy their journey home on the tram: the Blues lost 3-1! *W. A. Camwell*

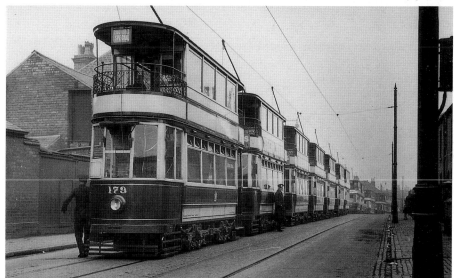

Right The standard type of tram to work on the Stechford route after 1939 was the 301 Class. Car 312 has worked a football special service and is returning to its home depot at Miller Street via Garrison Lane on its way from Stechford. On 20 September 1948, because of its poor condition, car 312 went to Coventry Road depot to replace other 301 Class trams that were to see further service, but it was broken up after the Stechford closure on 2 October.

The shopkeeper sweeping the pavement in front of his greengrocers shop is oblivious to the passing tramcar, but is perhaps bemoaning the lack of Saturday afternoon shoppers who might purchase his fruit and vegetables. As well as being fairly quiet as regards passing trade, there are only a few vehicles in the photograph of this junction at the Atlas public house. It is interesting, however, that all the visible cars and vans are manufactured by either Morris or

Morris Commercial, the latter's factory being in nearby Bordesley Green Road at Adderley Park. *A. Yates*

Above The Atlas public house was an important landmark at the junction of Garrison Lane and Cattell Road. It was here that the 84 route, from the city via Deritend, met the 90 route, which as we have just seen arrived via the more industrially lined back streets of Fazeley Street and Garrison Lane. Car 355 is seen negotiating the Atlas junction on Saturday 2 October 1948, the last day of tramcar operation on the Stechford service, and this tram's last day in service.

The Morris Fourteen Series II car of the mid-1930s is parked outside the greengrocers seen in the last photograph, in the short row of shops between Bangor Road and Crown Road. These were the only shops between Coventry Road and those around the junction of Bordesley Green and Bordesley Park Road, which was traversed by the Inner Circle bus route. *J. S. Webb*

Below On its way into the city via Cattell Road on the 84 route is car 336. It has just left the stop outside the Cleveland petrol station opposite the Atlas public house and has swung to the left at the junction. This tram would be another of the casualties of the Stechford route closure.

Unlike many tramway junctions, this one lacked any significant shops and as a result had all the hallmarks of being left behind by developers. It was too close to the main Small Heath shopping centre in Coventry Road to be really viable and it was at the fringe of an area of Bordesley that had been developed for industrial use.

The long row of houses beyond the tramcar in Cattell Road near the Atlas junction started a zone of transition from the mid-Victorian construction to the later, better-quality terraces further east along the route.

The Morris Fourteen car to the left appears in all the last three photographs and must have belonged to someone who worked or lived locally. *R. T. Wilson*

Bordesley Green

Right The Bordesley Green tram route opened for service on Saturday 24 November 1906, the same day that the depot opened on the corner of Arthur Street and Coventry Road. The initial allocation was of Brill Class cars, of which a total of 130 were delivered between 1905 and 1908. The first 50, numbered 21-70, had been delivered in two batches of 20 and 30 cars respectively by June 1906. They were standard UEC three-windowed, open-top-deck, unvestibuled trams with a seating capacity of 22 inside and 26 outside; they were mounted on Brill 21E trucks. The batch of 30 had Dick, Kerr DK6A 35 hp motors, making them slightly more powerful than the first 20. These little tramcars were only 27 ft 6 in long but could go anywhere on the system; thus they played a major part in opening and maintaining the plethora of new tram routes that were started by the Corporation in the 1906-07 period.

Seen at the junction of Bordesley Green and Victoria Street in about 1908, cars 43 (on the left and travelling out of city) and 44 were originally delivered to Rosebery Street depot, but were transferred to Coventry Road depot when it opened as part of the original allocation, thought to be cars 41-54.

Both trams were among the 54 Brill tramcars that were fitted in 1909 with the Maley track brake, after similar tram 22 overturned in Warstone Lane on 1 October 1907, killing two passengers.

Eventually top-covered and then vestibuled, both cars 43 and 44 lasted until early 1937 when, after the closure of the Stratford Road group of routes, they were among 43 of the Class rendered surplus to requirements. *Commercial postcard*

Right UEC open-balconied four-wheel car 322 trundles across the Bordesley Green-Victoria Street junction on its way out of the city when working the 84 route on the last day of operation of the Stechford routes. The first part of Bordesley Green could hardly be termed a shopping centre, but it did have a number of shops clustered around the corner site. The row of shops to the left of the Morris Eight overtaking the tram are those that were houses to the right of the view of car 43 in the previous photograph.

Fred Parkins hardware shop, with its galvanised buckets and basins, mops and brooms, overflows its wares on to the pavement on the far corner. Pearks Dairies shop is on the nearer corner; this was a Birmingham-based grocery chain with over 50 shops scattered around

the city belonging to an era before pre-packaging and supermarkets. Their shops had the smell of a grocers and provision merchants - there was the delicious heady smell of smoked bacon coming from half sides of pig hanging behind the Berkel slicer; butter was packed in grease-proof paper, as it had been hand-weighed from a recently delivered 56 lb tub; cheese had proper rind and came in huge circles; and sugar was weighed in blue bags - this, of course, presupposed that one had enough ration coupons to purchase these items. Food rationing had actually been increased in June 1947 and some of these items became very difficult to obtain for a number of years.

The mother, with her young daughter in her smartly styled coat, has just passed Barclays Bank, which was on the corner of Bordesley Green Road. This impressive two-storeyed building with a very high-pitched roof can be seen more clearly above the horse and cart in the previous photograph, which was taken about 37 years earlier. *J. S. Webb*

Left Beyond the Victoria Street junction the shops ended at Norwood Road, the junction of which can be seen just in front of the Ford Prefect E93A car to the right of the tram. This slight bend in Bordesley Green marked a brief zone of industry on the north side, with a metal merchants occupying the bombed site alongside the two lady pedestrians.

Car 380 is travelling out of town on the 90 route on a virtually deserted road; the remnants of wartime blackout restrictions can be seen on the lamp posts. This view is taken from the open balcony of an approaching 301 Class car and affords a good view of the overhead that supplied the electricity to the trams at a rate of 500 volts dc. The running wires were suspended over the track from the traction poles that had the usual attractive ornamental finials. The stringers were insulated from the running wire and the wire itself was divided into electrical sections of about half a mile in length; this enabled stretches of the line to be isolated at section boxes. *F. N. Lloyd Jones*

Left A slightly battered car, tram 337, looking a little worse for wear around the dash panels, leaves the passengers who have just alighted and accelerates away from the compulsory stop outside Bordesley Green Fire Station in 1947. The slightly Byzantine upper storey of the Fire Station contrasts oddly with the plainer casement windows of the ground and first floors. It was built in 1908 and although now used by a haulage contractor, the frontage has a preservation order placed upon it.

From here the tram route passed along Bordesley Green to the original terminus at Blake Lane; this area is also known as Little Bromwich. The first side road beyond the tram, about 200 yards away, is Fordrough Lane, but the next four roads lined with early-20th-century houses are Pretoria, Botha, Colonial and Churchill Roads, whose names celebrated the end of the Boer War in 1902.

Car 337 appears fairly full with passengers, with one person braving the outside balcony seat and resting against the wrought-ironwork. This tram would survive the Stechford abandonment, and was in fact repainted into post-war livery late in its career. *J. S. Webb*

Left On its inward journey into the city, car 315 has descended the hill from the original Bordesley Green terminus and has just passed Fourth Avenue. It is opposite the newsagents shop of Horace Field, which carries a large advertising hoarding for *John Bull* magazine, as well as one for Wills 'Star' cigarettes.

These four-wheeler 301 Class cars were used on the Stechford route from 1939 until its closure on 2 October 1948. This route was the last of Birmingham's tramway extensions to be built, and was on reserved track along Bordesley Green East to Stuarts Road. It was perhaps surprising that bogie cars did not use this modern extension, but as the 90 route went through the back streets of Digbeth it was considered that for normal service the clearances on some of the turns was too tight.

Car 315, devoid of advertisements, is working the 90 route during the last year of operation and would be broken up in October 1948. Had it not been for the outbreak of the Second World War, the 301 Class trams would probably have become extinct sooner; because of the hostilities its life was extended by eight years or so. *J. S. Webb*

Below left Six children run past the shops at the old Bordesley Green terminus without so much as a second glance at what the shops are selling. In the early post-war years the food rationing situation, if anything, worsened, and what in 1948 was regarded as a normal part of everyday diet would be considered by present-day children with horror.

To the right of the 30 cwt Bedford pick-up lorry is the greengrocers of Patrick & Bruce, who also sold fish as well as poultry and rabbit, the latter a somewhat less popular delicacy today. Behind the Bedford is George King's fish and chip shop, which, unlike the rabbit-seller, has survived to 1995 as Nic's fish and chip shop.

Car 316 is about to pull away from the Blake Lane compulsory tram stop on the last day of the Stechford tram services. It will pass the row of shops in Little Bromwich, which continued as far as Third Avenue, some three side roads down the hill from Blake Lane. *J. S. Webb*

Right The last day of operation of the Stechford trams was Saturday 2 October 1948. It was very much like every other day in the previous 42 years of working through Bordesley Green, but on Sunday morning the services would be replaced by new Daimler CVD6 buses from the 1756-1843 Class. Cars 340 and 308 pass in Bordesley Green at Blake Lane, just as 301 Class open-balconied trams had done since the spring of 1939. This was their last day of operational service for both of these 37-year-old trams, and both veterans would be consigned to the breakers' torch at Moseley Road depot.

The two young lady cyclists, whose bikes still have their rear mudguards painted white as a remnant of wartime blackout regulations, pass the parked 1939 two-door Austin Eight car. On the other side of the road is Jim Plumley's Austin K series 1½-ton pick-up lorry parked outside his building merchants premises, leaving just enough room for the descending tramcar to get by. The driver of the Morris Eight car is caught behind car 340, probably unaware that this is the last time that this misfortune will occur to him, on Bordesley Green at least! *J. S. Webb*

Right The standard pre-war allocation for the Bordesley Green routes were 71 Class cars. Cars 214, on the 84 route, and car 200, on the 90 route, stand opposite the shops at Blake Lane in Bordesley Green on 14 April 1938. Both of these ex-Mountain & Gibson Radial-trucked trams were fitted with Brush-designed Peckham P35 units in the late 1920s. With the exception of seven cars that were fitted with new top covers in 1923, the 71 Class cars could be easily recognised from the later 301 cars by their lack of balcony side screens. These were intended to prevent draughts coming down the stairs on to the platforms, and also give more protection to those hardy passengers who chose to ride on the open balconies. This does not seem to deter the five lads on the open balcony of car 214 from occupying that exposed position and grinning at the photographer.

Both trams, despite their apparently excellent condition, would be scrapped within 18 months of this photograph being taken and be replaced by 301 Class tramcars. *H. B. Priestley*

Right On leaving the former terminus at Blake Lane, the tram route to Stechford traversed some 600 yards of relatively straight track towards Belchers Lane. This was the first real opportunity for the tram drivers to open up the notches in their vehicles as they plied their way towards the Stuarts Road terminus. The route was lined with turn-of-the-century rows of terraced housing, which gave way on the southern side of this part of Bordesley Green to some early 1920s council housing. These terraced houses were superior to those in the inner part of the route, having bay windows and walled gardens, and marked the rapid expansion of Bordesley Green in the first decade of the century.

Behind the houses to the right of the tramcar was the Ideal Benefit Society's 'workman's garden colony', inaugurated in September 1908. Centred on Finnemore Road, running south-west from Bordesley Green, it had 225 houses and shops that were generously landscaped and with distinctive and varied housing styles. It postdated Bournville and was more utilitarian in style, but was itself soon overwhelmed by the enormous growth of council housing after the First

World War. Freshly repainted car 387 is working a football special service towards the city in 1948. *A. Yates*

Right Prior to the abandonment of the Yardley services, Coventry Road depot operated usually just over 80 trams, mainly from the 21 and 221 Classes of four wheelers. After the closure of the Yardley routes in January 1934, all of these Brill 21E-trucked cars were either transferred to Hockley or withdrawn. Car 70 went to Hockley until February 1937, when it was broken up. Trams from Highgate Road were redistributed around the system after the closure of the Stratford Road routes in January 1937 and this enabled nearly all of the three-bay-bodied trams to be taken out of service.

Car 70, the last of the 50 UEC cars numbered between 21 and 70 delivered in June 1906, was fitted with a Maley track brake in 1910. It is seen passing the Broadway public house at the end of Bordesley Green, working towards the city on the 90 route. Just visible is one of the seven members of the 71-220 Class, which were fitted with new top-covers in 1923 after wartime conversion to single-deck operation; it is probably car 166, which, along with cars 104 and 106, was allocated to Coventry Road depot at this time. These cars could always be distinguished by having canopy side screens on the balconies; this can just be seen above the Dewar's whisky advertisement. *A. D. Packer collection*

Below The view towards the terminus from the Belchers Lane-Bordesley Green junction was very different from the Victorian and Edwardian housing that had lined both the 84 and 90 routes for almost 2 miles. The extension from Blake Lane beyond the junction with Belchers Lane to Eastfield Road took place on Wednesday 4 November 1925. In retrospect, this extension seemed to have been built a little late. Although the vast tract of council housing beyond Belchers Lane in Bordesley Green East had only just been started, there was nearly half a mile of housing dating from before the First World War left unserved by public transport for 19 years.

Behind the 'Keep Left' sign on the traffic island are the houses that were part of the Batchelors Farm Estate. They were set out in groves and crescents and reflected the change of attitude to house-building that had been influenced by Ebenezer Howard's ideas on garden suburbs. Dating from 1925, the houses on the estate were, according to the *Birmingham Gazette*, being completed at a rate of six per hour! The estate, only a very small part of the Bordesley Green East development, contained about 700 Council-built properties. Birmingham Corporation built more council housing than any other local authority in England. Between 1924, when the Wheatley Housing Act introduced by the newly elected Labour Government tilted the scales in favour of council house construction, and 1939, Birmingham built just over 50,000 Council properties.

Just approaching the Belchers Lane island, through which it will pass, is car 365. It is working the inbound 90 route during the last year of operation and has just left the compulsory stop at the city end of the Bordesley Green East reserved track. *W. A. Camwell*

In April 1948 the Southern Counties Transport Society undertook a tour of Birmingham's tram system using the lightweight tramcar 843. The car had only been repainted in the 1946 livery the previous month, but already evident was the buckled side panels that indicated that the body frame was not in very good condition. Built by Brush in 1930, car 843 was Birmingham's last tramcar and it spent nearly all of its life working the straightforward Pershore Road routes, with very occasional forays on to Bristol Road. It was, however, used on special tours and to see it on Stechford's routes, the preserve of four-wheelers, was indeed unique. Later in June 1948, bogie car 522 worked a special tour, which also included the Stechford route.

The very full tram has just left Belchers Lane and is beginning to descend towards Alston Road on its way towards the Stechford terminus. Meanwhile a normal service tram, open-balconied car 388, climbs up the hill of Bordesley Green East on the 90 route service as a reminder of how tramcar design had progressed in the 18 years between their construction. *F. N. Lloyd Jones*

The steep descent from Belchers Lane alongside the Batchelors Farm Estate in Bordesley Green East can be readily appreciated in this view of car 388 seen from the balcony of a similar 301 Class car going towards the city. Car 388 has left the tall-chimneyed Broadway public house, on the skyline at Belchers Lane, and has passed Alston Road.

To the left of the photograph and behind the houses was the former Birmingham Fever Hospital, which for many years was the East Birmingham Hospital and was renamed the Heartlands Hospital on 1 April 1992.

All that can be seen from the balcony of the tram is one cyclist, seven pedestrians and three dogs, something that today on Bordesley Green East would be almost beyond belief! *D. R. Harvey collection*

The first request tram stop towards the city on the 1925 extension from Eastfield Road was at Kenwood Road. Car 144, seen at this stop on 1 April 1939, was already a 32-year-old veteran and had been allocated to Coventry Road depot since being displaced by 40 hp cars from the 512 Class at Highgate Road depot. Despite its excellent condition, the clear-out of 71 Class cars was scheduled form completion by the end of the year, when, had it not been for the outbreak of the Second World War, a start was to have been made on the later 301 and 401 Classes of four-wheelers. However, events on the international scene rather overtook the pre-war abandonment proposals, and this tram escaped the breaker's torch at West Smethwick by being one of the 22 members of the Class to be retained in case of emergencies. Therefore it almost survived the Second World War, being broken up in June 1945, although for the last five years of its career it had been standing by, awaiting a 'call-up' that never came, at **Rosebery Street depot.** *A. N. H. Glover*

Stechford

Left The last extension of any length of an arterial route in Birmingham was along Bordesley Green East to Stuarts Road on a reserved central track. It was opened on Sunday 26 August 1928 from the Ritz Cinema at Eastfield Road, and covered a distance of just over half a mile, most of which can be seen in the background as it passes across the River Cole valley and the adjacent playing fields. The Ritz, which can just be seen in front of post-war-liveried UEC-bodied tramcar 326, was opened on 7 November 1927 with a capacity of 1,442. After it closed on 29 September 1962 with *Detective Story* starring Kirk Douglas and Eleanor Powell, it was reduced to the indignity of becoming a bingo hall. The site today is an Aldi Supermarket, yet elsewhere in Bordesley Green East very little has changed.

There are no known photographs of trams at this 1925 terminus before the final extension. This view, taken in 1948, is also uncommon; it shows car 326 on the 90 route about to cross the gap in the carriageway at the Eastfield Road-Little Bromwich Road junction. *R. T. Wilson*

Left The valley of the River Cole was the least industrialised of all the rivers in Birmingham, being somewhat remote from the main markets and the supplies of raw materials from the Black Country. The Cole supplied power for 16 mills, most of which were active in the 18th century; this compares with 25 mills on the nearby River Rea, which the Stechford trams had crossed some 3 miles earlier. The Cole's mills were mainly grist-mils, but were later adapted to become industrial forges, and needle, wire and rifle-barrel works. The Hay Mill near Coventry Road made iron wire for the first Atlantic Ocean telegraph-cable link, which was laid by I. K. Brunel's great leviathan, the SS *Great Eastern*. The nearest mills to Bordesley Green East had been the Wash Mill upstream to the south, and downstream Stichford (or Stechford) mill.

The area between Hay Barns and Stechford remained open despite the siting of these mills, and, after falling into disuse, by the 1920s the land was not built upon but turned over to recreational space, which can be seen to the left of the photograph.

Four-wheeled car 322 has left the distant heights of the Stuarts Road terminus at Eastfield Road and is approaching a solitary passenger at the stop on the west side of the Cole valley in the early afternoon of Thursday 27 March 1947. Mary Webb, the late wife of the photographer, waits for the city-bound tram to take her into the city, or more probably to the next photographic location. *J. S. Webb*

Left Standing at the terminus at Bordesley Green East are three cars from the 301 Class. They are the prototype totally enclosed tram 342, an unidentified 301 Class car and, at the distant loading shelter, car 304 recently repainted in wartime grey. It is Easter 1942 and wartime restrictions also include the headlight masks and white-painted fenders, although by this time the wartime window blackout masks appear to have been removed. Coventry Road depot had acquired car 342 from Rosebery Street after the closure of the Oldbury group of routes at the end of September 1939. It had been kept in reserve, however, along with the other totally enclosed four-wheeler, car 347, for seven months before being transferred to work the Stechford services.

The distant tram, 304, was one of 18 grey cars, all from the 301 Class, that were allocated to Coventry Road during the war. Sixty-nine operational Birmingham tramcars were painted in this cheerless manner out of a service fleet of 448, about 15 per cent of the whole fleet and 55 per cent of the surviving 301 Class. *J. S. Webb*

The shops at the end of Bordesley Green East have remained remarkably unaltered. The end shop of the block is still a fish and chip shop and although the design has altered, there is still the facility to telephone from a call-box. MCW 'Metrobus' Mk II 2580 (POG 580Y) pulls away from the stop on the 96 route to Chelmsley Wood in July 1993.

In the intervening years the central tram reservation and terminus site have become just another dual-carriageway, although it is used as a car park. The dead-end beyond Stuarts Road has been removed and the road has been widened beyond the tram terminus site to the junction with the Outer Circle bus route in Stoney Lane, some 200 yards away. *D. R. Harvey*

On the eastern side of the River Cole, Bordesley Green East climbed gently towards the terminus. Just 200 yards before the terminus was the Richmond Road crossing. Richmond Road was used by the 36 bus route, which started its city-bound meander via Hay Mills, Tyseley and Sparkbrook from the nearby Yardley Fields Road. Inaugurated on 21 September 1936, this bus route served these predominantly industrial areas.

Cars 322 and 312 stand just below the terminus with the outbound car 322 on the 84 service loading up just as car 336, on the 90 route via Fazeley Street, starts to move away. Both 322 and 312 are still in the pre-war style of livery, while the third tram has been repainted in the less-ornate 1946 style. *R. T. Wilson*

Bogie cars were not usually seen on the Bordesley Green routes after the ex-CBT bogie-cars 451 and 452, nicknamed the 'Titanics', left Coventry Road depot in 1916. However, on 25 July 1948 car 522 operated an enthusiasts' tour that included the Stechford route. This tram had been rebuilt in 1929 along with nine others of the 512 Class with an eight-windowed, totally enclosed top-cover, and had its body strengthened in May 1948 with steel plates replacing the platform bulkhead windows.

In company with nine members of the 301 Class, including the ungainly 342, the much-modified GEC WT 32R 70 hp-equipped car 522 stands below the distant Stuarts Road terminus. The cars in the distance are outstabled from the depot, which during the summer of 1948 was being converted for motor bus operation. Service cars had to turn short at the specially installed crossover in the foreground.

The land to the right of the tramcar was later built on with low-rise flats, but with that exception the former terminus area remains much the same today. *D. R. Harvey collection*

Above The rare occurrence of the old with the new was difficult to capture on film, as the Stechford route's allocation of different tram classes changed very quickly in a matter of weeks in the spring of 1939.

The abandonment of the Hockley routes had far-reaching effects on the rest of the tram system. The decision had been made to withdraw 71 Class cars and replace them with the newer 301 Class cars which, by virtue of being 5 inches lower, had a better route availability. On the Stechford route the complement of 43 trams of the 71 Class would be replaced by the reallocation of 47 cars of the 301 Class, which themselves had been displaced by the ex-Hockley bogie cars.

The height difference in this unique view of 71 Class car 199 and 301 Class car 302 can clearly be seen as they stand at the Stechford terminus on 1 April 1939. Car 302 had been transferred by the end of February 1939 from

Witton to Coventry Road depot along with car 376 from Selly Oak, presumably to train the drivers on the slightly different 301 Class four-wheelers. Car 199 was only to last in service on the Stechford services until the following Thursday, and despite its apparent serviceable condition was placed in store by 24 May 1939 and broken up in the last month of peace. Interestingly, the older of the two UEC-bodied trams mounted on the 8 ft 6 in Brush Peckham P35 truck still displays the pre-November 1937 legal ownership of Birmingham Corporation Tramways & Omnibus Dept, as it has not been repainted since October 1934, while car 302 has the replacement Birmingham City Transport version. *A. N. H. Glover*

Below The conductor of car 369 at the Stechford terminus has turned the trolley-pole and is putting the trolley-head back on the overhead wire. The inverted

'V'-shaped trough just behind the trolley-head is where, at night, the driver attempted to estimate where the trolley-pole would be when it was to be turned for the return journey. The trough was designed to prevent sparks being seen from above when the tram was being reconnected with the power supply.

It is Easter 1944 and the prospect of opening up the Second Front in Europe was being awaited with interest. The advertisement on the tram, 'Victory will be sweeter with Mars', hints at this.

The tram, working the 84 route, is standing next to a typical BCT terminal shelter. This elaborate wooden structure was painted in the usual fairly uncompromising shade of dark green. Was this supposed to remind one of verdant pastures or primary school classroom doors? Behind the struggling conductor are the terraces of Stuarts Road, which were built around the first decade of the 20th century. The single-storey buildings to the left of the tramcar are those of the City of Birmingham Day Nursery, a wartime structure that reflected the need for child provision in view of the increase in war work being undertaken by women. *Burrows Bros*

BIRMINGHAM CORPORATION
TRAMWAYS TRAM DEPOTS

Albion (Holyhead Road, Handsworth)

Built for South Staffordshire steam trams. Opened 1885. Converted to electrics and re-opened 20.12.1903. Taken over by BCT 1.7.1911; closed 12.6.1912 on re-opening of Hockley depot. Leased to South Staffordshire 7.10.1912-31.3.1924. Used by BCT for parking trams on occasions of West Bromwich Albion home football matches. Capacity of 8 trams on 4 roads plus forecourt. Closed 2.4.1939. Used as industrial premises. Partially dismantled 1993 and re-erected at Black Country Museum, Dudley, 1995.

Birchfield Road

Built for Birmingham Central Tramways steam trams. Opened 11.1.1884. Used by BCT from 2.5.1907. Closed for trams 3.10.1924. Capacity 20 trams on 4 roads. Re-opened for buses 7.1.1925. Finally closed 19.8.1966 as operational garage and used for storage of withdrawn buses until 4.1967. Transferred to ambulance department as garage.

Bournbrook (Dawlish Road)

Opened by Birmingham Central Tramways for battery accumulator trams 24.7.1890. Converted to electric overhead 14.5.1901. BCT rented from CBT from 1.7.1911. Purchased 1.1.1912. Trams and buses from 19.7.1913. Capacity of 46 trams on 6 roads. Closed 11.7.27 and replaced by Selly Oak. Still in use as industrial premises.

College Road (Stratford Road)

City of Birmingham Tramways steam tram coke yard opened 1899. Converted to electric 1.1.1907 for PW use. Transferred to Public Works 10.4.1924.

Cotteridge

Built for City of Birmingham Tramways. Opened 23.6.1904. Capacity of 8 trams on 2 roads. Taken over by BCT 1.7.1911. Extended 1919-20 to capacity of 32 trams undercover on 8 roads, plus forecourt space. Closed for trams 5.7.52 and converted for buses. Closed by WMPTE 25 October 1986 and demolished.

Coventry Road (Arthur Street)

Opened 24.11.1906. Capacity 106 trams on 19 roads plus forecourt. Trams and trolleybuses from 7.1.1934. Closed for trams 2.10.1948, becoming bus and trolleybus garage until 30.6.1951. Converted to bus garage 1.7.1951. To WMPTE 1.10.1969. Closed 10.1985.

Henley Street Yard

Site used as collection point and PW yard alongside Birmingham & Worcester Canal. Lease on site began 26.3.1915. Closed 1946.

Highgate Road

Opened 25.11.1913. Capacity for 90 trams on 11 roads. Closed for trams 6.1.1937 and re-opened as bus garage 6.1.1937. Closed 14.7.1962 and transferred to the Fire and Ambulance service as main workshop.

Hockley

Built for Birmingham Central Tramways cable trams 1888. Closed 30.6.1911. Re-opened for electric trams 12.6.1912. Capacity of 88 trams on 8 roads plus forecourt. Closed for trams 1.4.1939 and converted for buses. To WMPTE 1.10.1969.

Kings Heath (Silver Street)

Birmingham Central Tramways steam tram depot, opened 1887. Capacity of 20 trams on 12 roads plus yard. Converted to electric by BCT by 1.4.1908. Closed c1911/1912. Site used as warehouse until 1970s. Demolished mid-1980s.

Kyotts Lake Road

Birmingham Central Tramways steam tram depot and works. Opened 5.1885. To BCT 1.1.1907. 8 roads in main works, 3 in bodyshop. Trolleybus overhauls from 1925-29 and 1934-51. Closed 8.1953 after last tram were broken up. Still in use as industrial premises.

Miller Street

Opened 4.1.1904 with capacity for 24 trams on 5 roads. Subsequent extensions enlarged depot to a capacity of 102 trams on 17 roads. Closed for trams 4.7.1953. Converted to bus garage. To WMPTE 1.10.1969. Closed by WMPTE 31.5.1986 but used by Central Coachways and later Your Bus.

Miller Street PW Yard

Opened 12.1908 and used as main Permanent Way yard with associated workshops and foundries. Closed 29.9.1952 and used for tram parking until closure for trams 4.7.1953. Used by buses from 5.7.1953. To WMPTE 1.10.1969. Closed by WMPTE 31.5.1986 but used by Central Coachways and later Your Bus.

Moseley Road

Opened 1.1.1907. Capacity of 77 trams on 15 roads plus forecourt. Closed for trams on 1.10.1949 and converted for buses. Closed by WMPTE 15.11.1975. In use as an indoor karting track.

Rosebery Street

Opened 14.4.1906. Capacity for 85 trams on 12 roads. Closed for trams 30.8.1947. Converted for buses. Closed by BCT 29.6.1968 and demolished.

Sampson Road

Opened 1925 and used as paint shop until 1939. Used for storage from summer 1939. Closed when lease expired 9.1945.

Selly Oak

Opened 12.7.1927 for trams and buses, replacing Bournbrook. Trams only 20.6.1928-1.1.1935. Capacity for 80 trams on 10 roads plus forecourt. Closed for trams 5.7.52. Closed by WMPTE 2.8.1986 and used as vehicle store. Planning permission for housing granted 1995.

Washwood Heath

Opened 1.1.1907. Capacity for 66 trams on 11 roads plus small forecourt. Nechells trolleybuses introduced 27.11.1922. Buses after 15.1.1923 until 28.10.1925. Trolleybuses withdrawn 30.9.1940. Trams and buses after 19.8.1946. Closed for trams from 1.10.1950. To WMPTE as bus garage 1.10.1969.

West Smethwick

Built for Birmingham & Midland Tramways steam trams. Opened 5.1885. Converted to electric tram operation 24.11.1904. Capacity under cover for 44 trams on 11 roads plus extensive forecourt. Taken over as operating depot from Birmingham & District by BCT 1.4.1928. Closed 30.9.1939. Demolished c1961.

Witton

Built by Birmingham & Aston Tramways for steam trams. Opened 1882. Converted to electric trams 6.10.1904. Taken over by BCT 1.1.1912. Capacity for 38 trams on 7 roads. Closed from 1.10.50 except for storage and scrapping. Re-opened as out-station to Miller Street 30.11.1952. Closed 4.7.1953 and used for scrapping trams until 8.1953. Sold to Dents and later to Thomas Startin as car showroom. Re-opened 1988 as Aston Manor Transport Museum.

Yardley

Opened for City of Birmingham Tramways 1904. Acquired by BCT 1.1.1912. Closed c1912/1913. Used as car showrooms until c1964 then demolished.

INDEX OF STREET NAMES AND TRAM ROUTES

Figures in (brackets) are route numbers. Words in CAPITALS are terminal points and areas of Birmingham.

ACOCKS GREEN (44) 77, 78
Adderley Street (12, 14-22, 44-45, 56-58, 82-84, 91) 78
ALBERT STREET (11-13, 17, 19, 42-45, 56, 58, 82, 84, 91) 73, 74, 76-78, 82-83
Allison Street (12-13, 17, 19, 42-45, 56, 58, 82, 84, 89, 91) 75
Alston Road (84, 90)
Aston Brook Street (1-2, 63-64, 78-79) 42
ASTON CROSS (1-2, 63-64, 78-79) 42

Bangor Road (11-12, 84, 90) 90
Barwell Road (11, 90) 87
Bath Row (33-34) 10
BEARWOOD (29, 34) 13, 27-29
Bearwood Road (29, 34) 13, 28-29
Beeches Lane (34) 13
Belchers Lane (84, 90) 93-95
Birmingham Road (74-77) 62-63
Birmingham Road (87) 40
Birmingham Street (87) 36-37
BLACK LANE (75) 67
Blake Lane (11-12, 84, 90) 82-83, 92-94
BOLTON ROAD (22) 55, 79
Booth Street (23, 28, 74-77) 60
BORDESLEY (12-13, 17, 19, 44-45, 56, 58, 82, 84, 89, 91) 77-79, 81-87
Bordesley Green (11-12, 84, 90) 82-83, 87, 90-94, 96-97
Bordesley Green (84, 90) 92, 94-97
Bordesley Green Road (-) 89, 91
Bordesley Park Road (22) 79-80, 90
Botha Road (11-12, 84, 90) 92
BOURNVILLE (-) 93
Bradford Street (4, 18, 20-21, 42-43, 48, 50, 67, 83) 76
Bristol Road (35, 69-72) 21, 54, 65, 95
Bromford Lane (-) 37, 64-65
Bull Ring (12-13, 17, 19, 42-45, 56, 58, 82, 84, 91) 75, 77
Bull Street (-) 49, 73
Burnt Tree (74, 87) 38, 40, 70-71

Camden Street (-) 19
Camp Hill (17-21, 44-45, 82-83, 89, 91) 78-79
CANNON HILL (37) 43
Cape Hill (29-30, 87) 25-27, 30
CARTERS GREEN (73-76) 5, 65-67, 69, 71
Castle Hill, Dudley (-) 41, 71
Cattell Road (12, 84) 81-82, 90
CHARFORD, BROMSGROVE (-) 34
Chester Road (2) 43
Church Square, Oldbury (87) 36
Church Street, Oldbury (87) 37
Churchill Road (11-12, 84, 90) 92
City Road (29, 30, 87) 24
Claremont Road (23, 25-28, 74-77) 55
Coles Lane (-) 67
College Road, Handsworth (-) 20
College Street (-) 20
COLMORE ROW (23-28, 73-77) 44, 48-50, 59
Colonial Road (11-12, 84, 90) 92
Congreve Street (29-32, 55, 80, 85-88) 18-19
Constitution Hill (23-28, 74-77) 50-52
Cornwall Street (-) 17, 49
Coventry Road (13-16, 22, 56-57, 84) 76, 78-81, 88, 90-91, 97
Cranford Street (31) 22
Crocketts Road (23, 28, 74-77) 44
Crown Road (11-12, 84, 90) 90
Curzon Street (11, 90) 83, 87

Dale End (3, 3X, 6-10, 13, 15, 17, 19, 42-45, 48, 50, 56, 58, 67, 82, 89, 91) 42, 73
DARLASTON (-) 60, 63, 68-69
DARTMOUTH SQUARE (74-77) 64
Dawson Road (26) 58
Deritend (12, 14-22, 44-45, 56-58, 82-84, 91) 76-77, 82, 90
Digbeth (12, 14-22, 42-45, 48, 50, 56-59, 82-84, 89, 91) 75-77, 92
DUDLEY (74, 87) 31-34, 36, 38-41, 50, 61, 66-67, 71
Dudley Port (74) 69-70
Dudley Road (29, 31, 55, 80, 85-88) 18, 20-21, 23-25
Dudley Road East (87) 38
Dudley Road West (87) 38

Eastfield Road (84, 90) 94-96
EDMUND STREET (29-32, 55, 80, 85-88) 17-18
ERDINGTON (2) 42
Ethel Street (29) 28

Farm Street (23, 26-28, 74-77) 53
FAZELEY STREET (11,90) 74, 82-85, 90
Finnemore Street (-) 93
Five Ways (33-34) 10-12
Floodgate Street (-) 76
Fordrough Lane (11-12, 84, 90) 92
Fountain Road (34) 13
Fourth Avenue (11-12, 84, 90) 92

Garretts Green (-) 78
Garrison Lane (11, 90) 82, 86-90
Garrison Street (-) 86
George Street (29-31, 87) 19
George Street, Lozells (5, 24-25) 52
Glover Street (11, 90) 85
Granville Street (-) 10
Gravelly Hill (2, 5, 63, 78-79) 42-43
Great Barr Street (11, 90) 84-87
GREAT BRIDGE (74,77) 41, 50, 66, 69
Great Charles Street (23-28, 74-77) 51
Great Hampton Street (23, 25-28, 74-77) 51
Great King Street (23, 25-28, 74-77) 51
Grove Lane (29-39, 86-87) 18,24-25, 33
Grove Lane, Handsworth (26) 56-60

Hagley Road (34) 10-13, 20, 55
Halesowen Street, Oldbury (87) 37
Halfords Lane, West Bromwich (-) 62
HALL GREEN (17-18) 74
Hamstead Road (24-25) 55
HANDSWORTH (23, 26-28, 74-77) 62, 71
Harborne Road (-) 10
HAWTHORNS (23, 74-77) 65-70, 62
Hawthorn Street (87) 33
Heath Street (31) 21, 23
High Street, Birmingham (12-13, 17, 19, 42-45, 56, 58, 82, 84, 89, 90) 73, 75
High Street, Bordesley (12-13, 17, 19, 44-45, 56, 58, 82, 84, 89, 91) 78
High Street, Cape Hill (29-30, 86-87) 26-27, 30-32
High Street, West Bromwich (74-77) 64-65, 67
Highgate Road (4, 17-21, 42-45, 82-83) 13, 54
Hill Street (38-40, 47, 51) 9, 43, 76
Hill Top (75) 66-68
Hockley Brook (23, 25-28, 73-77)
Holloway Bank, Wednesbury (75) 68
Holloway Head (33-36, 69-72)
Holly Road (26) 58

Holmes (North, South, East and West) (11, 90) 88-89
Holyhead Road (23, 28, 74-77) 61
Holyhead Road, Wednesbury (75) 68
Horse Fair (33-36, 69-72) 10

Icknield Street (29-31, 85-88) 19, 23
Islington Row (33-34) 10
IVY BUSH (34) 12
Ivy Street (-) 86

John Bright Street (33-36, 46, 53-54, 69-72) 9, 10

Kenwood Road (84, 90) 95
Kenyon Street (23, 26-28, 74-77) 50
KINGS HEAD (34) 11-13, 29
Kingston Hill (13-16, 22, 56-57, 84) 79-80
Kitts Green (-) 78
Kyotts Lake Road (-) 43

LADYWOOD (33) 20, 23-24
Ladywood Road (33) 10
Lawley Street (11, 90) 86
Lee Bank Road (-) 10
LIVERY STREET (23-28, 74-77) 48-51
LODGE ROAD (32) 18-20
Lower High Street, Wednesbury (-) 68
LOZELLS (24-25) 48, 50
Lozells Road (24-25) 52
Lozells Street (-) 52

Margaret Street (29-32, 55, 80, 85-88) 17
Market Place, Oldbury (86-87) 36-37
MARTINEAU STREET (3, 3X, 6-10) 42, 73
Maxstoke Street (11, 90) 87
Miller Street (1-3, 6, 60, 78, 79) 42, 89
Montague Street (11, 90) 85
Monument Road (34) 12, 19
Moor Street (12-13, 15, 17, 19, 42-45, 48, 50, 56, 58, 67, 82, 84, 89, 91) 74-75, 82
Moseley Road (40-43, 47-48, 50-51, 67) 43, 76, 82, 86, 93

NAVIGATION STREET (New Street Station end) 34, 37, 41
NECHELLS (7) 55
New Birmingham Road (-) 71
New Canal Street (11, 90) 83
NEW INNS (23, 28, 74-77) 48, 50-51, 57, 60-61
New Street, West Bromwich (73-77) 65
Newhall Hill (29-32, 55, 80, 85-88) 19
Newtown Row (6) 42
Nova Scotia Street (-) 56

OLDBURY (86-87) 31-34, 36-37, 39-41, 64, 71, 97
Oldbury Road (86-87) 32-33, 35
Oxhill Road (26) 51, 55, 59

Parade (29-31, 55, 80, 86-87) 19
Paradise Street, West Bromwich (74-77) 64
Park Street (11, 90) 83
Pershore Road (36, 46, 53) 95
Plough & Harrow Road (34) 12
Pretoria Road (11-12, 84, 90) 92

Queens Drive (-) 9
Queens Head Drive (23, 28, 74-77) 60

Rabone Lane (31) 22
Rea Street (14, 16, 18, 20-22, 42-43, 48, 50, 57, 83) 75-77
REDNAL (70) 40-41

Richmond Road (84, 90) 96
Roebuck Lane (-) 32
Rookery Road (-) 59
Rosebery Street (-) 10-12, 19-26, 33, 91

ST ANDREWS (11, 90) 81, 87, 89
St Michaels Street (74-77) 64-65
St Pauls Road (86) 19, 24, 32
Sampson Road (-) 76
Sandon Road (34) 12-13, 28-29
Sandwell Road (-) 59
SELLY OAK (35, 69-72) 51, 98
Seymour Street (11, 90) 83
Shireland Road (29-30, 86-88) 27
SHORT HEATH (78) 42
Short Heath Road (78) 42
SMETHWICK (86-87) 27, 32-33, 71
Snow Hill (23-28, 74-77) 49-50
SOHO (31) 22
Soho Hill (23, 26-28, 74-77) 53, 55
Soho Road (23, 26-28, 74-77) 56-57, 60
Soho Street (31) 22
Spon Lane (74-77, 86-87) 18, 20-21, 33, 64
Stafford Road (23, 26-28, 74-77) 74, 91
STECHFORD (84, 90) 74-76, 83-84, 86, 88, 93, 96, 98
Steelhouse Lane (2, 78, 79) 49
Stockland Green (1-2) 42
Stoney Lane (86-87) 31
Stoneyhurst Road (79) 43
Stony Lane (-) 97
Stratford Road (17-21, 44-45, 82-83, 89) 74, 91
Streetly Road (78) 42
Stuarts Road (84, 90) 92-93, 96-98
Suffolk Street (33-34, 69-72) 9
Summer Hill Road (29-31, 55, 80, 85-88) 19
Summer Row (29-31, 55, 80, 85-88) 19
SWAN VILLAGE (74) 69
Sydney Street (11, 90) 87-88

Telford Way (-) 32
Templefield Street (12, 84) 82
Third Avenue (11-12, 84, 90,) 92
Three Shires Oak Road (29) 28-29
Tilton Road (12, 84) 82, 89
Tipton Road (87) 38
TIVIDALE (87) 38-39, 71
Tividale Street (87) 39
Tollhouse Way (-) 31-32
Tyburn Road (79) 42-43

Union Row (26) 58
Unity Place (87) 36

Venetia Road (11, 90) 88-89
Victoria Street (11, 90) 91
Villa Cross (5, 24-25) 52
VILLA PARK (3, 3X) 86

WALSALL (-) 69
Warstone Lane (32) 54
WASHWOOD HEATH (10) 86
Waterloo Road (29-30, 86-87) 26-28
Watery Lane (-) 79
WEDNESBURY (75) 5, 34, 50-51, 63-64, 66-69
WEST BROMWICH (74) 34, 40-41, 62-66, 68, 71
WEST SMETHWICK (87) 33-35, 38
Wheeler Street (24-25) 48, 52
Whitmore Street (-) 5, 53
WINDMILL LANE (30, 86-87) 18, 22, 26-30
Winson Green Road (-) 23
WITTON (3, 3X) 43, 98
Wolseley Street (11, 90) 87

YARDLEY (15-16) 78, 94
Yardley Fields Road (-) 96